FOOD

FOR YOUR

BROOD

Sam Gates

Photography by Anthea Kirkman

FOOD
FOR YOUR
BROOD

Author's acknowledgements

Huge thanks to:

Andrew for your encouragement, inspiration and love.

My wonderful army of enthusiastic supporters and top testers:
Stormer, Lulu, Carol, Stefan, Georgia, Mum, Dad, Polly, Daisy and
Emma, the Pattinsons, Ned and Oscar, Helen, Julia, Claudia,
Penny, Kerry, Karen, Holly and Ruby.

The supermodels: Jack Storm, Tallulah, Rachel, Kate-Ruby, Amy,
Jordan, Carol, Ed, Diani, Maggie, Shirley, Max, Teia, Kate,
Kiera, Kai and Josh.

Quirky me, Sonja Moore, Laidback, Mariaan van Zyl, Le Creuset
and Klobbabags for props.

My unflappable and hardworking helpers: Magda, Plackie,
Tanya, Gloria and Wendy.

Linda de Villiers, Joy Clack and Helen Henn at Random House
Struik, for making it happen.

And to the amazing and talented Anthea Kirkman, for your
stunning photography and boundless enthusiasm.

Published in 2015 by Struik Lifestyle
(an imprint of Random House Struik (Pty) Ltd)
Company Reg. No. 1966/003153/07
Estuaries No. 4, Century Avenue
(Oxbow Crescent), Century City, 7441
P O Box 1144, Cape Town 8000, South Africa

Visit **www.randomstruik.co.za** and
subscribe to our newsletter for
monthly updates and news.

Publisher: Linda de Villiers
Managing editor: Cecilia Barfield
Editor and indexer: Joy Clack
Designer: Helen Henn
Photographer: Anthea Kirkman
Food styling: Sam Gates and Anthea Kirkman
Proofreader: Gill Gordon

Reproduction by Hirt & Carter Cape (Pty) Ltd
Printed and bound by Craft Print International
(Pty) Ltd, Singapore

Contents

Introduction

I love the different meanings of the word 'brood'. It's such a perfect way to describe your favourite people: the family and friends who are always on your side, sharing love and laughter when the sun is out and hanging around in darker times. They play a fundamental and essential role in our lives, so it's no surprise to me that the Afrikaans word *brood* means 'bread', the simplest, most basic meal of all. Like staple foods, broods are a crucial factor for survival and happiness, and the best meals are always those shared with the people you love.

Growing up, food burst vibrantly into life for me when we left the city and moved to the country. Before that, it had functioned as fuel in the form of joyless, overcooked school dinners or as a rather inconvenient interruption to the business of being a kid. But our new place had stacks of cool neighbours with children the same age, and overnight the whole family gained a busy social life that revolved around food. We roamed between houses in a sprawling posse of kids, grazing our way through impromptu picnics, communal teas and braais, and being fed by random parents whenever we stood still for long enough.

We were having a ball and so were the grown-ups. At night our parents joined their new friends in a frenzied round of entertaining that coincided with the latest food trends. World cuisine was in and thrilling dishes surged out of kitchens at breathtaking speed, bypassing dull dining rooms without a backwards glance. Pointless etiquette and tedious dinner parties were booted out of touch, along with fish knives, side plates and blancmange, and quickly replaced with amazing food that demanded to be eaten hot, fast and anywhere you could find space to stand up.

We snuck downstairs in our pyjamas to spy on raucous parties where hordes of happy people talked, laughed and downed steaming, colourful bowls of fragrant curries, spicy stir-fries and richly flavoured tagines. I quickly realised that sharing meals was infinitely better than eating alone and now that it's my turn to cook for the crowds, a noisy group around the table is always my favourite accompaniment.

But finding divine culinary inspiration or the time to be creative when you are cooking for family and friends every day can be difficult, so when the kids asked me to write a book of recipes for sharing I knew it had to be bright and adventurous, but still practical. That's why *Food for your Brood* is all about creating exciting everyday food as well as sparkling meals for big gatherings and events, be it indulgent sugar-rush holidays, quick pit stops on the road or a cosy night in at club duvet. Whatever the reason for your crowd to come together, you'll find the perfect recipe here to complement the occasion and help fuel, nurture and treat those close to your heart. Just make sure they're really hungry...

Sam Gates

Best breakfasts

Breakfast is quintessential *Food for your Brood* that should take you to lunch and beyond. During the week, burnt toast or a quick bowl of cereal might suffice, but come the weekend it's time to gather your people together for long, lazy breakfasts that smack of holidays, lie-ins and delicious anticipation of the downtime ahead.

This chapter uses traditional ingredients and some hardworking new ones to help you create exceptional morning feasts. I've nothing against a classic fry-up, particularly if someone else is cooking, but have always found cooking is more fun off-road, so these dishes are a long way from the full English. Just remember to stick to foods that feel like morning, rather than those that veer towards lunch. Gruyère and Emmental cheeses are heavenly first thing, but I'd leave their runny, pungent relatives – Brie, Camembert and the like – until later in the day. Likewise, ham and chorizo make a fine breakfast, but save chicken or lamb for lunch or later.

Vegetarian breakfasts can't rely on the salty fallback of bacon or sausages and have to work harder to be interesting, but even they still have no-go zones. It's fine to include spinach or leeks but you won't find many turnips or celeriac at dawn.

A clean breakfast plate is full of promise and optimism, and a crowded, noisy table sharing opinions, gossip and laughter is a blissfully blank canvas for you to fill with fabulous food. Whether it's filling boots for a monster day ahead or feeding hangovers, a perfect breakfast gives you the opportunity to put things right and send your honeys out well prepared and ready to tackle whatever the day may bring.

Retro cheesy eggy bread with roast tomatoes and salty ham

Eggy bread is no-frills food and none the worse for it. White bread triangles dipped in beaten egg and fried make for a definitive camp breakfast, and nothing tastes better to hungry kids drunk on fresh air than soggy slices of eggy bread dripping with tomato sauce.

But these sunshine-yellow slices of freedom don't travel well and when you try to sell the same meal at home, minus the tents and scorched campfire pans, it becomes nothing more than plain old fried bread (and a bit too, well, eggy at that), which no one is very keen on eating.

Luckily, the plus side of being back from the bush is that you'll be closer to a decent supermarket, and with the help of some Swiss cheese, decent tomatoes and a crusty baguette, you can quickly elevate this simple pleasure into a seriously substantial breakfast. Invest in the thinnest, saltiest ham you can find to serve alongside, and your table will soon fill up with punters. It might have needed an image revamp, but eggy bread is back. **Feeds 4**

2 branches of cherry tomatoes on the vine
30 ml (2 Tbsp) olive oil
Salt and freshly ground black pepper
4 eggs

30 ml (2 Tbsp) milk (or fresh cream if you're feeling luxurious)
50 g Parmesan cheese, finely grated
30 ml (2 Tbsp) chopped chives

15–45 ml (1–3 Tbsp) butter
1 baguette, cut into thick slices
12 slices Parma ham, prosciutto or other thinly sliced salty ham
Small handfuls of rocket

Heat the oven to 180 °C.

Place the tomatoes on a baking tray, drizzle with the olive oil and season well. Bake for 20–30 minutes until they are soft and starting to ooze, then switch the oven off, cover the tomatoes with foil and return to the oven. Place a heatproof platter in the oven to warm up.

Beat the eggs in a large bowl and add the milk, cheese and chives, plus lots of black pepper.

Melt the butter in a nonstick frying pan until hot. Dip the slices of baguette in the egg mixture until well coated and soggy, then place several in the frying pan. They will start sizzling straight away. Cook for 3–5 minutes on each side until they turn golden brown but not burnt. Set aside to keep warm and place the next batch in the pan. Keep going until you have cooked them all, adding more butter between batches if needed.

Take the warm platter out of the oven and arrange the tomato branches alongside a pile of the bread slices and a mountain of artfully draped ham. Add a pile of rocket and eat immediately.

Baked egg bar

Baked eggs are ideal breakfast fodder for big groups who won't agree on what to eat. So rather than let things descend into an unseemly squabble, create a colourful distraction with this pick 'n' mix-style counter. Each guest just needs to grab a ramekin, egg, a sprinkle of their favourite toppings and everyone will be happy, including you.

Baked eggs are best cooked in a *bain-marie*, which sounds technical but all you do is heat the oven, add boiling water to a deep roasting pan and you're ready to go. Having eaten too many overcooked baked eggs in the search for the optimum cooking time, I've learnt that you need to preheat the oven exactly and don't be tempted to leave the eggs in beyond the times below, even if they look wobbly. Eggs are sneaky little blighters that cook at alarming speed once they start, leaving you with a dusty, disappointing centre if you don't whip them out on time.

If you are planning on doing all the options below, ramp up the quantities and prepare the fillings in advance (better still, get the breakfast guests to help). Then, when they are ready, give everyone their ramekins and let them go. **The quantities below are per person**

Butter
10 ml (2 tsp) fresh cream
1 egg
Salt and freshly ground
**   black pepper**

Spinach, Gruyère and chilli
15 ml (1 Tbsp) cooked spinach, chopped and drained, 15 ml (1 Tbsp) finely grated Gruyère cheese and 1 ml (¼ tsp) finely chopped chilli

Mushroom, garlic and thyme
2 mushrooms, thinly sliced and gently sautéed in butter with 2.5 ml (½ tsp) crushed garlic and a sprinkle of fresh thyme leaves

Sun-dried tomato and rocket
7.5 ml (½ Tbsp) finely grated Parmesan cheese, 5 ml (1 tsp) chopped sun-dried tomatoes and 15 ml (1 Tbsp) chopped rocket

Creamed leek and chorizo
30 ml (2 Tbsp) finely chopped leek, fried gently with finely chopped chorizo

Prosciutto and truffle oil
15 ml (1 Tbsp) shredded prosciutto and a dribble of truffle oil

Cheddar, ham and chutney
15 ml (1 Tbsp) finely grated Cheddar cheese, 15 ml (1 Tbsp) finely chopped ham and 7.5 ml (½ Tbsp) chutney

Heat the oven to 180 °C.

Generously butter a ramekin or small ovenproof bowl. Spoon in your chosen filling (reserve a little for sprinkling on top), plus 5 ml (1 tsp) cream. Carefully crack an egg into the ramekin and add another 5 ml (1 tsp) cream. Sprinkle the reserved filling over the top and season well.

Place all the ramekins in a deep baking tray or roasting pan. Carefully pour boiling water into the tray or pan until it reaches halfway up the sides of the ramekins. Place in the oven and bake for 10–12 minutes. Remove and eat immediately with hot, crusty bread and a teaspoon.

Double-smoked bacon on *roosterbrood* with chilli jam

As any camper knows, bacon tastes best when cooked outside, where its sweet saltiness is intensified by wood smoke and a drop of fresh air. We took things up a notch recently on an overnight mountain trip, when we stayed in a rustic shelter off the grid. There was only a two-sided fish grill and a fire pit by way of kitchen equipment, but what we did have was flour and yeast from the farm shop, and thanks to the resident ex-Cub Scout in our group, a roughly remembered recipe for *roosterbrood* (griddle cakes). There's something that feels so right about making your own bread on a campfire. It turns the most basic, domestic cooking into an altogether more adventurous exercise.

There are an infinite number of ways to make *roosterbrood*, but they all seem to work. One friend uses a kilogram of flour to make 24 rolls while another uses the same quantity to make six (some people are just hungrier I guess).

For double smokiness, use heavily smoked bacon to start with, and when your fire is at the burning ember stage, braai lightly, flick-flacking the grill to cook each side evenly. Then, after you've worked up an appetite from the fire building, kneading and grilling, invite your friends over to share the best bacon sandwiches on the planet. Take along some homemade Helluva hot tomato and chilli jam (see opposite) and you'll be in breakfast heaven. **Makes 12 good-sized bacon rolls**

1 x 10 g sachet instant dried yeast	400 ml lukewarm water	Helluva hot tomato and chilli jam (see recipe opposite)
15 ml (1 Tbsp) sugar	1 kg white bread flour	
30 ml (2 Tbsp) olive oil	5 ml (1 tsp) salt	
	20 slices good smoked bacon	

My top tip is to prepare the dough before you build your fire, as it will take about 1 hour to rise. Then, when you have shaped the *roosterbrood* into rolls and it is rising again, make your fire.

To make the *roosterbrood*, mix the yeast, sugar and oil with 45 ml (3 Tbsp) of the water in a jug. Mix the flour and salt in a large bowl, make a well in the centre and pour in the yeast mixture followed by 150 ml water. Stir well as it starts to form a dough. Keep adding the water until it's used up, stirring and kneading until you have a gorgeous smooth and silky dough which isn't too dry or wet. Place in an oiled bowl and cover with a clean dishcloth or plastic wrap. Leave to rise until doubled in size (about 1 hour).

Empty the dough onto a generously floured surface, roll into a big rectangle and cut into 12 even squares. Leave space between the squares and set aside to rise again until doubled in size.

Now get your fire going. Dust the rolls with flour and put on a grid over hot coals. It mustn't be too hot or the outside will burn before the inside cooks, so watch them like a hawk and turn over after 5 minutes. Keep turning the rolls until they sound hollow when you tap them.

Lay your bacon in the fish grill and close tightly. Cook over hot coals and then pile onto the rolls. Serve with a big dollop of the tomato and chilli jam. It's going to be a beautiful day.

Helluva hot (and not) tomato and chilli jam

Until you get the hang of setting points, making preserves feels best left to those who've been shown the way of the jam by mysterious elderly relatives. Don't panic though, as this isn't really a jam in the fruity sense of the word, and requires no special gifts or talents, just patience, a liquidiser and the desire to have some in the fridge. The only downside is that it's strangely addictive, so unless there's a fresh batch ready, you won't want to finish a jar, even if all that's left are the sticky bits at the bottom.

Try varying the chilli quota until you find your comfort zone. Alternatively, keep two jars in the fridge – a taste bud-searing helluva hot, and a gently spicy and tangy number.

250 g ripe tomatoes, cored and roughly quartered, seeds left in
4 red chillies for the not-so-hot or 2 Scotch bonnets or habaneros for the helluva hot version
4 cloves garlic, roughly chopped

10 ml (2 tsp) chopped fresh ginger
30 ml (2 Tbsp) fish sauce
100 ml red wine vinegar
300 g castor sugar, golden if you have it
250 g ripe tomatoes, finely chopped into 5 mm dice, seeds left in

Blend the roughly quartered tomatoes, chillies, garlic, ginger and fish sauce to a fine purée in a blender.

Place this purée in a saucepan and add the vinegar and sugar. Bring to the boil slowly, stirring all the time. When it boils, turn down to a gentle simmer and add the finely chopped tomatoes. Skim off any foam and cook gently for about 1 hour, stirring every 5 minutes or so to release any solids that settle on the bottom. I use a bendy spatula for this so you can constantly scrape the mixture from the sides and bottom of the saucepan and it cooks evenly. Don't be tempted to boil it furiously, this takes love and patience.

When you get to a lovely, thick, jam-like consistency, pour the mixture into sterilised jars and allow to cool to room temperature before sealing. When open, store in the fridge, where it will happily keep for a few weeks.

Broodsters avo, egg, sweet chilli and cheese breakfast wrap

Wraps are unbeatable for those who hate crusts or, more importantly, for those needy mornings when you crave taste and texture but have to rely on something else to hold it all together. Wraps may look like orderly, tidy parcels, but cut through the velvety folds and you'll find a satisfyingly mad jumble of your favourite foods within. Let's face it, at breakfast, who knows what the day will bring, so it makes sense to grab everything you might need and roll it all up in one package.

Wraps need to be strong enough to take everything you're going to throw at them, yet soft and pliable enough to envelop bulky contents without breaking, so use big, dinner plate-sized wraps rather than roti-style ones which don't bend well. Wrap rolling is an art form which takes practice, but follow my instructions and you'll soon be turning out these tight little bundles of joy.

In this vegetarian beauty, avocado mash creates a cool base for chilli, cheese and other goodies piled high to make one enormous wrap. It will feed two if you're unlucky enough to have to share, otherwise it makes a mega treat just for you if no one's looking.

1 egg
5 ml (1 tsp) butter
1 large white wrap, the biggest you can find
½ ripe avocado, gently mashed
60 ml (4 Tbsp) grated mature Cheddar cheese
1 tomato, diced
Small handful of rocket, chopped, plus a few leaves for serving
15 ml (1 Tbsp) sweet chilli sauce
Salt and freshly ground black pepper

Whisk the egg in a bowl. Gently melt the butter in a small pan. Add the egg and cook until loosely scrambled and not too dry. Set aside.

Lay out the wrap and dollop the mashed avocado in a horizontal rectangle on the lower half. Using the back of a spoon, smooth it out, leaving a clear 3–5 cm margin from the edges.

Place the scrambled egg on top of the avocado, and sprinkle over the grated cheese, diced tomato and chopped rocket. Drizzle over the sweet chilli sauce in zigzag lines and season.

Fold in the two sides of the wrap, until they almost touch, but not quite. With the sides folded, start rolling the wrap up from the bottom. Use your thumbs to bring up the bottom of the wrap and carefully roll it over the filling and folded sides. Tuck in the corners as you go and press the sides in, creasing the whole package tightly as you roll. You will end up with a neat, tightly wrapped parcel. If you like your cheese melted, pop the parcel into the microwave for 30 seconds at this point.

Set on a plate with the seam underneath, carefully cut in half and serve with the two cut sides balanced on top of each other and a few extra rocket leaves sprinkled on the top.

Gruyère and spring onion hotcakes with poached eggs

Pancakes and hotcakes (flapjacks) are big in our house for lazy weekend breakfasts, but they're not always sweet. Cheese is the key to turning out the perfect specimen, and the stronger and more determined the better. Throw in a handful of sharp spring onions and you'll end up with these fluffy, fighting hotcakes. They also work well as a side to traditional fry-ups if you want an alternative to fried potatoes or hash browns.
Feeds 4

350 g cake flour
10 ml (2 tsp) baking powder
2.5 ml (½ tsp) salt
2 eggs, separated
350 ml full-cream milk
15 ml (1 Tbsp) olive oil
80 g Gruyère cheese, finely grated
20 g Parmesan cheese, finely grated
6 spring onions, very finely chopped
Salt and freshly ground black pepper
15–45 ml (1–3 Tbsp) butter
4–8 eggs for poaching

Sift the flour, baking powder and salt into a bowl and stir well.

Whisk the egg yolks, milk and oil until blended. Add the grated cheeses and spring onions and pour it all into the dry ingredients, then stir well to make a smooth batter. Season generously with lots of salt and pepper. Whisk the egg whites until stiff, then fold into the batter, keeping as much air in as possible.

Melt 15 ml (1 Tbsp) of the butter in a frying pan and, when it's sizzling, ladle a few tablespoons of batter into the pan. Cook gently until golden brown, and then flip onto the other side and cook until golden again. Remove from the pan and set aside somewhere warm until you have finished the batter.

Poach the eggs, drain and serve on top of the warm hotcakes with lots more salt and black pepper, and an optional sprinkling of something green on top for colour.

Big fat waffles with marshmallows, chocolate and cream

If you've already recoiled in horror at the thought of all of these pieces of kiddie dreams gathered together on one plate, I do understand. It's not often that chocolate and marshmallows should make up the first meal of the day. It's not wholesome, it's not healthy, and it's certainly not for term time, but there are occasions when nothing else will do. I'm talking about the first day of school holidays, big celebrations, or special birthday breakfasts for a small (or large) person. In essence, those rare, wonderful days when you can legitimately order a total mobilisation of all that is sweet.

I'm very particular about waffle quality control as shop-bought waffles are invariably horrid bits of cardboard that dissolve quickly, whereas a decent homemade version will fill your kitchen with wafts of vanilla and turn a simple sugar fest into top treat food. It's worth investing in a waffle iron as they aren't expensive and make the cooking process a complete breeze, but you can also fry these in a frying pan like a drop scone.

I find that the batter is better after sitting for a while, so try to make it the night before and refrigerate, covered in plastic wrap. I use an electric mixer, but you can do the job just as well with a strong arm, making sure there are no lumps in the finished batter. **Makes enough for about 20 waffles**

125 g butter
100 g castor sugar
2.5 ml (½ tsp) vanilla essence
2 large eggs, beaten
250 g cake flour
5 ml (1 tsp) baking powder

250 ml milk
100 g chocolate, dark is often better as milk
    chocolate makes things just too, too sweet
150 ml whipping cream
100 g marshmallows, mini or otherwise
Silver edible glitter if you're feeling sparkly

Cream the butter until fluffy, and then add the sugar and vanilla essence. Mix in the eggs until smooth, then gradually stir in the flour and baking powder. Stir in the milk and beat quickly until smooth. Leave to rest for at least 1 hour or overnight.

When you are ready to eat, cook the waffles in a waffle iron according to your machine's instructions, then keep warm.

Bring a saucepan of water to the boil, turn the heat down to a gentle simmer and place a heatproof bowl over the top of the saucepan, making sure it doesn't touch the water. Break the chocolate into the bowl and watch as it melts, stirring as little as possible.

Whip the cream until stiff and fluffy and set aside.

Plate the waffles, spoon over whipped cream and sprinkle with marshmallows. Take the melted chocolate bowl off the saucepan and drizzle zigzags of chocolate over the cream, marshmallows and waffle. (Alternatively, create a stack of waffles, chocolate, cream and marshmallows.) Sprinkle with glitter, serve to the hungry hordes, and make sure there's open space nearby to accommodate the sugar rush afterwards.

Sweet potato and leek cakes with homemade baked beans

Breakfast is when you get to indulge and this, the most substantial of my morning recipes, takes that very seriously as it swerves into brunch, lunch and even light supper territory. Size-wise, think of these less as fritters and more as fish cakes or burgers and you'll realise that today is the day you definitely won't be going hungry.

Sweet potato makes a hefty hash-type base with a soft, comforting denseness, but if you have only white potatoes, make them anyway. The cakes are great for mopping up a rich bean stew, and mine is inspired by the classic Boston baked beans. The original beans had to be boiled in molasses for hours but, luckily for us, canned beans work just as well, and with chorizo instead of bacon, and pomegranate molasses, it's divine. Make the beans the day before, and don't be suprised if they turn out a whole lot darker and more dangerous than any beans you've ever known. Trust me, it's a good thing. **Feeds 8**

Homemade baked beans
15 ml (1 Tbsp) olive oil
150 g diced chorizo
2 cloves garlic, crushed
1 large red onion, finely sliced
1 carrot, peeled, sliced and finely diced
3 x 400 g tins chopped tomatoes
15 ml (1 Tbsp) tomato paste
5 ml (1 tsp) smoked paprika
2.5 ml (½ tsp) dried or 15 ml (1 Tbsp) chopped fresh oregano
30 ml (2 Tbsp) brown sugar
10 ml (2 tsp) wholegrain mustard
2 x 400 g tins beans (cannellini beans, haricot, black-eyed, butter, borlotti, etc.), rinsed
Salt and freshly ground black pepper

Sweet potato and leek cakes
500 g orange-fleshed sweet potatoes, peeled and cut into 2.5 cm chunks
500 g potatoes, peeled and cut into 2.5 cm chunks
40 g butter
2 cloves garlic, crushed
1 fresh red chilli, finely chopped
1 ml (¼ tsp) fennel seeds
120 g leeks, halved and finely sliced
30 ml (2 Tbsp) chopped fresh parsley
2.5 ml (½ tsp) salt
Lots of freshly ground black pepper
Cake flour for dusting
Butter or olive oil for frying

To make the baked beans, heat the oil in a heavy-based saucepan and cook the chorizo quickly until golden. Turn the heat down and add the garlic, onion and carrot, frying gently until translucent. Add the tomatoes, tomato paste, paprika, oregano, sugar and mustard and bring to the boil. Turn the heat down and simmer for 40–50 minutes, stirring frequently until the sauce is rich and thick. Add water if it's too dry.

Pour in the drained beans and warm through. Season with lots of salt and pepper and set aside until needed.

To make the sweet potato and leek cakes, steam all the potatoes for 12–15 minutes until soft, then leave to drain in a colander for 1 hour. It might seem ages but the sweet potato will be wet and soggy if you don't. Add the potato chunks to a mixing bowl and stir gently, breaking up the chunks into smaller lumps, without mashing them.

Melt the butter in a small frying pan and add the garlic and chilli. Cook for 3–4 minutes before adding the fennel seeds. Give it a stir and add the sliced leeks and cook softly without burning for 10 minutes.

Add the leek mixture to the potatoes along with the parsley, salt and pepper and stir through gently. Using floured hands, form the mixture into eight cakes and dust with flour. Place onto a floured plate until they are all made, then cover with plastic wrap and refrigerate for at least 30 minutes.

When you are ready to cook, heat a knob of butter or 15 ml (1 Tbsp) olive oil in a frying pan until hot and fry for about 6 minutes each side until crisp and golden. Remove and keep warm while you cook them all.

Place two cakes on each plate with the beans on the side (or serve the beans in a small pot or cup if you're feeling fancy).

Super skinny tomatoes on toast with drizzly Bovril

There are times in life when we need to go easy and live a little more tentatively. It could be after a mammoth New Year's Eve, a significant birthday or simply when the dust has settled after a holiday full of feasts and fat chewing.

Times of culinary reflection need a slo-mo approach to the fridge, but that's oh so dull, which is why resolutions are often just that. The answer is to turn to this flibbertigibbet of a breakfast. It's light as a feather but packs a punch of salty flavour that won't leave you feeling grumpy and short changed. **Feeds 2**

2 big, ripe, juicy beef tomatoes, stems removed and cut into thick slices (discard the top and bottom slices which tend to be mostly skin)
2 slices chunky bread, preferably seeded and with lots of substance (don't even think about using a thin sliced loaf. I'm not a bread snob, but a sliver of white will turn into a soggy rag almost instantly)

40 ml (8 tsp) Bovril
Freshly ground black pepper
Optional: olive oil (if you need strength)

Heat the grill to medium.

Lay the tomato slices on a grill pan covered with foil and place under the heat for 8–10 minutes until cooked but not soggy. Remove and keep warm.

Place the bread under the grill and toast lightly on one side. Remove, turn over and spread a thin layer of Bovril on the untoasted side. Lay the tomato slices over the top, covering as much of the bread as possible. If you need to cut them a bit to fill in gaps, then do so.

Drizzle more Bovril over the tomatoes, back and forth in wobbly stripes. I use about 5 ml (1 tsp) per slice of bread here, but use more if you like it strong. Slide back under the grill and watch carefully. You want the tomatoes to cook and soften without setting the edges of the toast on fire. When the tomatoes are looking soft and mushier, remove them from under the grill and you should be able to gently pull off the skin from around each slice.

Sprinkle with black pepper, drizzle with olive oil if using and eat while still hot.

Superhero soups

Despite all my efforts to be an organised super woman type, I still seem to spend far too much time rustling up rush-hour meals from random ingredients. Creating decent food from weird combinations of leftovers and cupboard remnants can be strangely reward-ing when it works, but if the pickings are particularly thin, as long as you have stock or tomatoes remember that soups are particularly forgiving on the empty-handed cook. Fresh stock is ideal, but cubes or concentrate will also do fine, just remember to season the soup only when it has reduced and the flavours have become concentrated.

I'm not a big fan of watery consommés, preferring my soups to function as proper meals, so these recipes are for rich, thick and flavoursome broths that provide instant satisfaction and keep you going until the next meal. If you're not in a mad panic, make them in advance when you have some downtime – they will all keep well in the fridge for a couple of days. It's not just useful to have everything ready for the next rush hour, but the dicing, chopping and stirring is oddly soothing, and brings calm and order to crazy family days.

Best tomato soup in the world

As frugal students we lived on tinned tomato soup, which bore little resemblance to the real thing, but it was a vaguely edible, cheap meal. Over time we even became strangely fond of its acid burn and fluorescent orange colouring, but after landing in the real world with a proper pay packet, the love affair abruptly ended.

During a particularly foul winter years later, I decided to make a proper tomato soup and it was so delicious I can't believe I wasted good eating time on those horrid tins. It's so easy to make and all that chopping and wafts of garlic and basil floating around always puts me in a great mood (in fact, I think I need to go and make some right now!).

As a soup it's amazing enough, but it also has other talents. Reduce it and you have a rich, flavoursome sauce for pasta or pizza. Make lots and freeze some for the days when the fridge is bare and you need a quick topping. **Feeds 4**

Roasted tomatoes
45 ml (3 Tbsp) olive oil
12 big ripe tomatoes, halved horizontally
3 cloves garlic, crushed
2 handfuls fresh basil, shredded
5 sprigs fresh thyme, leaves removed, no stalks
Salt and freshly ground black pepper

Soup
2 medium-sized red onions
45 ml (3 Tbsp) olive oil
Pinch of chilli flakes if you like a bit of heat
2.5 ml (½ tsp) dried or 5 ml (1 tsp) fresh
   thyme leaves
2 x 400 g tins chopped tomatoes, plus 1 tin water
15 ml (1 Tbsp) honey
Salt and freshly ground black pepper to taste

Heat the oven to 200 °C.

To make the roasted tomatoes, paint a little of the olive oil in a shallow baking tray. Lay the tomatoes on the tray, cut side down. If you have one of those brilliant gadgets for taking out the eyes of the tomato, use it, as it will save you time later. Or use a knife. You will end up with a tray of tomato-ey speed bumps.

Sprinkle the crushed garlic, basil and thyme over the tomatoes, then drizzle with the rest of the olive oil. Grind salt and pepper over the tray and place in the oven for 30 minutes.

While the tomatoes are roasting, make the soup. Peel the onions, cut in half and slice as thinly as you can. Place the olive oil, onions, chilli flakes (if using) and thyme in a big, heavy-bottomed saucepan and fry very gently, without browning, until the onions are soft and translucent. Remove from the heat.

Check on the tomatoes. If they are sunken and soft, and the skins have shrunk, take them out and allow to cool. As soon as you can touch them, gently remove the skins by lifting them off, like a hat. Put all the tomato skins into a sieve and press down with a spoon so you can catch as much juice and flesh as possible.

Pour the roasted tomatoes, juice and all, from the baking tray into the onions. Add the juice from the sieved skins and stir well. Add the tins of chopped tomatoes and a can of water, as well as the honey. Season well.

Slowly bring to the boil. When it starts boiling, turn the heat down to a simmer and leave for 40–50 minutes, stirring every now and then. If it looks too thick, add a little more water.

Take off the heat, season to taste with salt and pepper and add a little more honey if it tastes too sharp. I like my soup chunky and rustic but if you prefer it smooth, give it a whizz with a stick blender. Serve with crusty bread and a sprinkle of extra basil.

Spicy carrot and lentil hybrid soup/stew

My early fervent hatred of lentils was entirely due to the piles of burnt, tasteless, yellow lumps dumped onto our plates by grumpy dinner ladies at school. They were so grim I avoided them completely for the next two decades, until a friend served up her signature lentil soup at a birthday dinner, and I didn't have the heart to refuse. It was amazing and resulted in a sea change in attitude to these excellent little pulses.

Armed with my new outlook, I went lentil crazy, experimenting with stacks of recipes, but none bettered this deep and meaningful hybrid soup/stew. It's pretty, filling and guaranteed to leave you glowing and ready for whatever the day will bring. Be warned, it does rely on a good blast of chilli to pep it up, but you can omit that if you're not a fan, as the other spices still bring warmth and depth to the mix. **Feeds 4 easily for lunch with a warm naan bread or two**

30 ml (2 Tbsp) butter
15 ml (1 Tbsp) vegetable oil (not olive)
2 medium-sized red onions, finely sliced
3 cloves garlic, crushed
2 carrots, peeled and coarsely grated
5 ml (1 tsp) cumin seeds
5 ml (1 tsp) yellow mustard seeds

5 ml (1 tsp) black mustard seeds
10 ml (2 tsp) turmeric
300 g split red lentils
2 x 400 g tins chopped tomatoes, plus 2 tins water
10 ml (2 tsp) grated fresh ginger
5 ml (1 tsp) finely chopped fresh red chilli (optional)
5 ml (1 tsp) salt

1 ml (¼ tsp) freshly ground black pepper
Juice of 1 lime
1 x 30 g punnet fresh coriander, chopped

Heat the butter and oil in a heavy-bottomed saucepan and fry the onions and garlic until translucent. Add the grated carrots, cumin seeds, yellow and black mustard seeds and cook for 2 minutes before adding the turmeric. Cook for another 2 minutes.

Add the lentils and tinned tomatoes, then fill up the tomato tins with water and pour that in too. Finally, stir in the grated ginger, chilli, salt and ground black pepper. Bring to a simmer and cook very gently, uncovered and stirring frequently, for 40–50 minutes until the lentils have melted and all but dissolved. This soup sticks easily so watch with beady eyes, and if the lentils are still crunchy, add extra water.

When the lentils are soft and yielding, but before they turn into mush, take the saucepan off the heat, allow to cool and add more seasoning if necessary. I always find it needs lots of salt. Before serving, add the lime juice and sprinkle with lots of chopped fresh coriander. This is always better eaten warm rather than piping hot.

White bean and onion soup with fresh thyme

Sweet caramelised onions floating around in beefy soup is the signature look for classic French onion soup, which is traditionally made with a rich meat stock.

My lighter version uses chicken stock instead and adds white beans for substance and satiety. Don't be deceived by its anaemic appearance, as this is a remarkably good soup with a depth of flavour that tastes as if you've been boiling bones for hours, instead of sprinkling in a stock cube or two and flitting about the kitchen like a lightweight (which is what you will have been doing). **Feeds 4**

60 g butter

1 kg onions, sliced as thinly as you can or using the slimmest processor blade

7.5 ml (½ Tbsp) yellow mustard seeds

15 ml (1 Tbsp) chopped fresh thyme leaves

45 ml (3 Tbsp) cider vinegar

1.5 litres (6 C) hot chicken stock

1 x 400 g tin cannellini beans, drained

1 short baguette (the kind you use to make a sandwich), sliced very thinly

60 g Gruyère cheese, finely grated

45 ml (3 Tbsp) fresh cream

Salt and freshly ground black pepper

Chopped fresh parsley for serving

Melt the butter in a large saucepan and cook the onions very s-l-o-w-l-y. You want them to soften and caramelise without browning. It might take up to 30 minutes, but this is where the magic happens, so be patient.

Add the mustard seeds and cook for a few minutes, then drop in the thyme and vinegar. Turn up the heat until the vinegar has been absorbed. Add the hot stock and bring to the boil slowly, before reducing the heat to a gentle bubble and allowing it to tick over for 30 minutes.

Pour in the beans and heat through, then mash with a potato masher in the saucepan, not to a pulp, just until the colour starts to lighten and you don't have any whole beans, just lots of nice crunchy lumps. Turn the heat down low to keep the soup warm.

Heat the oven grill. Lay thin slices of baguette on a grill pan, drizzle lightly with olive oil and slide under the hot grill until golden. Turn over and sprinkle with grated Gruyère. Pop back under the grill until melted, then remove and keep warm. Take the soup off the heat and swirl the cream through it . Season to taste with salt and pepper and sail the cheese toasties on the top, scattered with a glittering of parsley.

Perfect pea soup with Parma ham

Frozen peas are basically cooked as far as I'm concerned, and boiling them can quickly turn them into hard little bullets. Far better to just place them in a sieve and pour boiling water over the top until they are just defrosted, sweet and crisp.

As well as being the perfect green vegetable, peas also make substantial fillings for pies, quiches and tarts, and this, the fastest, creamiest soup ever. It takes only a few minutes to throw together, but the result is a smart and serious starter or lunch. Although it will benefit from a decent homemade stock, it's happy enough with a stock cube if you're in a hurry. **Feeds 4 hungry lunchers**

4 slices Parma ham (or 50 g finely chopped pancetta)
30 ml (2 Tbsp) butter
1 medium-sized white onion
500 g frozen peas
Handful of basil leaves
750 ml (3 C) hot chicken stock
100 ml fresh cream
Salt and freshly ground black pepper

Fry the Parma ham until crispy. Break into small pieces and set aside.

Melt the butter in a saucepan and gently sauté the onion until translucent. Add the peas, basil and hot stock, bring to the boil and immediately turn down the heat to a very gentle simmer for about 5 minutes. Take off the heat and blend to the smoothest texture your machine will give you.

Return the soup to the stovetop, on a medium heat, and add the cream until warmed through – don't let it boil. Season to taste with salt and pepper and serve sprinkled with the Parma ham.

Pear and blue cheese soup

On a chilly autumn day with rain splattering the windows, a group of us were sprawled around the table of a self-catering cottage, dissecting the excellent wedding party that had happened the night before. No one fancied venturing to the shops in the dismal deluge outside, so hungry, hungover and in need of comfort, we foraged in the kitchen instead. The fridge was pretty bare but we did manage to ferret out the scraggy end of a bit of Stilton, an onion and some slightly dodgy pears. Not exactly rich pickings but with the help of three dusty stock cubes from the cupboard it was transformed into a magical soup that cut through the gloom like a blast of balmy sunshine.

With access to a full cupboard, I've refined the recipe since then, but it's still a suprisingly sophisticated soup, treading a sublime balance between the sweetness of caramelised pears and the off-kilter sharpness that blue cheese brings. If you make it in advance, make sure you reheat it very slowly without boiling.
Feeds 4

15 ml (1 Tbsp) butter
1 red onion, finely chopped
4 big juicy pears (don't use hard ones), cored, peeled and finely chopped
1 litre (4 C) chicken stock
100 g Stilton or other crumbly blue cheese, crumbled or chopped up very small
Salt and freshly ground black pepper
Squeeze of fresh lemon juice
Chopped fresh chives or parsley for garnishing

Melt the butter in a medium, heavy-bottomed saucepan and cook the onion until translucent. Add the finely chopped pears and stock, and bring to the boil before turning down to a simmer. Let it gently bubble away until the pears are very soft, which will take around 20 minutes.

Liquidise or blend the soup until smooth, then return it to the saucepan and heat gently without boiling. When it's hot, start adding the blue cheese, a little at a time, and stir each addition so it dissolves completely in the soup.

Taste and season well with salt and pepper (it seems to need a fair amount of salt) and if it's too sweet, add lemon juice. Sprinkle over the chopped fresh herbs (or extra blue cheese) before serving with slices of warm baguette.

Light lunches and sublime suppers

Holiday lunches and supper times are the ideal opportunity for celebrations and mega-feasts, with plenty of time to linger over mountains of food (and search for somewhere to have a crafty snooze afterwards). But if you prefer to take it a little easier when you draw breath and refuel before the afternoon or evening blasts in, why not try these lighter culinary pit stops instead.

Pre-kids, lunch and supper can be a sporadic affair. Sometimes it happens, sometimes it doesn't, depending on the demands of the day. But when kids arrive, they need regular feeding, regardless of your time or enthusiasm, and haphazard catering just won't cut it anymore. The good news for you is that lunch anchors the middle of the day, allowing time for a brief stocktake in the same way that a baby's bath time draws a curtain on the turbo-charged experience of living life at the pace of small people. Likewise you can rediscover the joy of supper, which heralds the welcome end of the day and is somehow a happier, breezier meal than dinner. Perhaps it's because you've done your bit for the world and your family, and you're home until morning, so all that's left is to kick back and ease into the evening with a plate of food and your favourite people.

What works best for both these mealtimes are dishes that are fresh, filling and won't drag you down, and if they can be made in advance, so much the better. Simple lunches and suppers may not be the headline acts, but as they make up most of our weekly meals there's no excuse for them not being appetizing. These recipes are a long way from a cheese sandwich, but are the answer to light meal conundrums, whether you're looking for a book club supper, a smart lunch for the in-laws with birdie appetites, or a tableful of toddlers.

Seventies-style red peppers stuffed with spicy rice

Seventies cookbooks are full of cheery gingham tablecloths and stuffed peppers posed alongside straw-clad Rioja bottles. Pretty enough, but in reality most of those peppers were leaky, bitter towers that didn't hold their shape. An unlikely candidate for a comeback, perhaps, but if you get them right, these butter-soft treasure chests are delicious, slicing open like juicy steaks to reveal a tasty, golden filling, ideal for lunch or a light supper.

To guarantee success, use the sweeter red or orange peppers and choose those with a flat base so they sit well rather than lurching drunkenly around the plate. You also need to ensure your filling packs a taste punch so don't be shy with spices, seasoning and sauce. This super-spicy stuffing was inspired by a trip to Istanbul, but unlike classic Turkish stuffed peppers, these are served hot. **Feeds 4, and useful if you have vegans or vegetarians around**

160 g basmati rice
100 g grated courgettes
5 ml (1 tsp) salt
60 ml (4 Tbsp) olive oil
1 large onion, finely chopped
2 cloves garlic, finely chopped
2.5 ml (½ tsp) turmeric
5 ml (1 tsp) ground cumin
5 ml (1 tsp) garam masala
5 ml (1 tsp) ground coriander

Generous pinch of cayenne pepper
½ fresh red chilli, finely chopped
2 small tomatoes, finely diced
60 ml (4 Tbsp) chopped fresh coriander plus more for sprinkling
Freshly ground black pepper
400 ml water
4 big, fat, square red peppers
Olive oil for drizzling

Heat the oven to 180 °C.

Wash the rice well, drain and set aside. Place the grated courgettes in a colander and sprinkle over the salt. Set aside.

Heat the olive oil in a large frying pan and sauté the onion and garlic until cooked but not brown. Add the turmeric, cumin, garam masala, ground coriander, cayenne pepper and chilli and cook for 2 minutes. Pour in the rice and cook gently, stirring all the time, for 6–8 minutes so the rice is well coated.

Add the courgettes and stir, then add the tomatoes, fresh coriander, a generous grind of pepper and the water. Simmer gently for about 12 minutes, until the rice is nearly cooked. Don't cook any longer as you are going to be putting it into the oven.

Slice the tops off the peppers and scoop out the seeds. Fill with the cooked rice and courgette mixture and put the lids on the top. Place in a casserole dish small enough for the peppers to sit snugly next to each other and drizzle over a little olive oil. Bake for 1 hour, basting with the juices several times during cooking.

Golden onions baked with cheese and herbs

There are two schools of thought when it comes to baked onions. Cook them whole and pour sauce and cheese over the top, or get fancy, scoop out the middle and fill them up with goodies before baking. Both are good but the simple version has the added bonus of providing excellent mopping up juices to play with, so make sure you have a loaf of crusty bread handy. **Feeds 4 for lunch or 8 as a side dish**

8 medium-sized onions, peeled and the top and bottom sliced off
30 ml (2 Tbsp) olive oil
15 ml (1 Tbsp) chopped fresh thyme
2 cloves garlic, finely chopped
Salt and freshly ground black pepper
50 g Parmesan cheese, finely grated
2.5 ml (½ tsp) smoked paprika
250 ml fresh cream
4 slices wholewheat bread, whizzed into breadcrumbs
15 ml (1 Tbsp) chopped fresh parsley or thyme

Heat the oven to 190 °C.

Bring a large saucepan of salted water to the boil and blanch the onions for 6 minutes. Drain and cut in half horizontally, then fit them, cut side up, into a greased gratin dish or shallow casserole. They should fit snugly and hold each other upright. Drizzle with olive oil, scatter over the chopped thyme and garlic, season with salt and pepper, then bake for 30 minutes.

Meanwhile, mix the Parmesan, paprika, cream and a good grind of salt and pepper in a bowl. Stir in the breadcrumbs.

Take the onions out of the oven and pour the cheese, cream and breadcrumb mixture over the top. Return to the oven for another 20 minutes until the sauce is bubbling and golden.

Remove from the oven and serve from the hot dish sprinkled with fresh parsley or thyme.

Herby wrapped kingklip with mustardy spinach

This combination of salty pork-wrapped fish, cool baby spinach and firm waxy potatoes makes for a fresh, summery lunch or supper. Here we're using my favourite fish, a meaty flaky kingklip, but you can use most firm white fish or even salmon. It looks and feels like a big meal, but can be made easily in 30 minutes.
Feeds 4

30 ml (2 Tbsp) butter, at room temperature
30 ml (2 Tbsp) finely chopped fresh chives, plus
   a handful of whole chives
15 ml (1 Tbsp) finely chopped fresh parsley
2 cloves garlic, crushed
Zest of 1 lemon
8 slices prosciutto

4 x 100 g kingklip fillets, skin removed
15 ml (1 Tbsp) lemon juice
Salt and freshly ground black pepper
600 g small waxy potatoes
250 g baby spinach leaves, rinsed
30 ml (2 Tbsp) wholegrain mustard
15 ml (1 Tbsp) olive oil

Heat the oven to 180 °C.

Beat the butter, fresh herbs (except the whole chives), garlic and lemon zest together. Line a baking tray with foil, then lay out the slices of prosciutto. Place each piece of kingklip in the centre of two slices. Spread a quarter of the herb butter over each piece of fish, then drizzle a little lemon juice over and season with salt and pepper. Take both ends of the prosciutto slices and scrunch or 'tie' them over the centre of the fish. Slide a few whole chives under the 'knot' of prosciutto.

Place the potatoes in a saucepan of salted water and bring to the boil. They will need to boil for 10–15 minutes until tender, so when they are almost done, put the kingklip into the oven and set a timer for 12–15 minutes.

Meanwhile, as soon as the potatoes are cooked (which should be before the kingklip is ready), drain, peel and slice them into thick coins. Place back into the warm saucepan and cover.

Heat a large frying pan or wok and add the spinach, shaking to turn it over. When it is starting to wilt, add the mustard, olive oil, and then the warm, cooked potatoes. Season to taste and serve with the kingklip.

Deep purple salmon and dill gravadlax with dill and mustard sauce

This gravadlax is the tastiest and prettiest of my no-cook lunches and very useful if you're staying somewhere off the grid. The beetroot adds colour rather than flavour, in the form of a deep purple frill around the edges of the salmon.

This dish takes a few minutes to prepare, then needs to be left somewhere cool and safe from bugs and predators for up to 48 hours. Add thinly sliced bread and a dollop of homemade mustard and dill sauce for a beautiful starter or light lunch. **Feeds 4**

500 g skin-on salmon fillet, as chunky as possible, bones removed
2 small cooked beetroot, grated
40 g coarse sea salt
50 g castor sugar
5 ml (1 tsp) crushed coriander seeds
1 ml (¼ tsp) fennel seeds
1 x 30 g packet fresh dill, stalks and all, finely chopped

Cover a flat baking tray with plastic wrap and place the fillet, skin side down.

Combine the grated beetroot, sea salt, sugar, seeds and chopped dill in a bowl, then spoon the mixture on top of the salmon. Using your hands, press the mixture all over the fish so you can't see any orange flesh, then wrap two layers of plastic wrap tightly over the whole tray. Place a chopping board on top and stack tins or weights on top. You are aiming to squash the salmon evenly to allow the colour from the beetroot to seep in.

Place the tray in the fridge or anywhere cold and leave for 24–48 hours, then unwrap, drain and gently wipe the marinade off the salmon. Carefully slice very thinly before laying in overlapping slices. Serve with the dill and mustard sauce.

Dill and mustard sauce
⅓ x 30 g packet fresh feathery dill leaves, finely chopped
45 ml (3 Tbsp) wholegrain mustard
15 ml (1 Tbsp) runny honey
15 ml (1 Tbsp) cider or white wine vinegar
120 ml (8 Tbsp) sunflower or other vegetable oil (not olive)
Salt and freshly ground black pepper

Mix all the ingredients together, except the oil and seasoning, then slowly whisk in the oil 15 ml (1 Tbsp) at a time until you have a smooth dropping sauce. If it's a little cloying, add a couple of drops of lemon juice or more vinegar. Season to taste.

Lamb and hot harissa meatballs

This is a simple tomato sauce with meatballs that goes brilliantly with couscous, rice or pasta. Lamb makes an excellent dense meatball, which holds together well and absorbs flavours without collapsing. Some carnivores hate the thought of diluting their meat, but a slice of bread soaked in milk makes the meatball lighter and smoother.

Harissa is a fiery North African paste that brings a depth of flavour rather than a searing blast of heat, and it works so well with lamb that I even sneak it into traditional roast lunches. This is my father's recipe and he uses fennel rather than traditional caraway seeds, and adds sun-dried tomatoes for richness. It lasts for ages, so make a big jar and keep it in the fridge to add to sauces, stews or mayonnaise.

Make the harissa paste up to a week ahead, then the tomato sauce (which can also be made up to two days in advance, then stored in the fridge), and the meatballs on the day you eat. **Feeds 4**

Hellishly hot harissa with sun-dried tomatoes
12 big dried chillies
3 cloves garlic, crushed
2.5 ml (½ tsp) salt
60 ml (4 Tbsp) olive oil
5 ml (1 tsp) coriander seeds
2.5 ml (½ tsp) cumin seeds
2.5 ml (½ tsp) fennel seeds
2.5 ml (½ tsp) hot smoked paprika
4 sun-dried tomatoes in oil, drained

Soak the chillies in hot water for 10 minutes. Remove stalks and seeds. Blend chillies, garlic and salt with the olive oil, add the remaining ingredients and blend to a paste. Add more oil if it's dry. Taste, and add one more sun-dried tomato if you want to calm things down.

Tomato sauce
30 ml (2 Tbsp) olive oil
1 medium onion, finely chopped
2 cloves garlic, crushed
2 x 400 g tins chopped tomatoes
2.5 ml (½ tsp) salt
Freshly ground black pepper
5 ml (1 tsp) hellishly hot harissa (see recipe above)
2 handfuls of fresh basil leaves, chopped

Heat the oil and gently fry the onion and garlic for 10 minutes until translucent. Add the tinned tomatoes, salt, a good sprinkling of pepper, the harissa and basil and simmer away gently for 40–50 minutes, stirring from time to time until the sauce is thick and rich. While the sauce is simmering away, get cracking on the meatballs.

Lamb meatballs

1 slice wholewheat bread, torn into little pieces
 and soaked in 125 ml (½ C) milk
45 ml (3 Tbsp) finely chopped fresh mint
30 ml (2 Tbsp) finely chopped fresh coriander
1 clove garlic, crushed

1 egg yolk, beaten
5 ml (1 tsp) hellishly hot harissa (see recipe
 opposite)
500 g minced lamb
Olive oil for frying
Handful of torn basil leaves for serving

Line a large baking tray with greaseproof paper.

Drain the bread and place in a large mixing bowl. Add the mint, coriander, garlic, egg yolk and
harissa and stir well. Roll your sleeves up, add the minced lamb and squidge and squodge
the mince through your hands to ensure it is evenly mixed through the herbs and spices. Roll
the mixture into walnut-sized balls and place on the baking tray at equal distances apart in
pleasing symmetrical lines. You can cover these with plastic wrap and leave in the fridge for a
few hours before cooking if you need to, but take them out and bring back to room temperature
before proceeding.

Heat a little olive oil in a large frying pan until hot, then add the meatballs in a spiral so they
are not invading each other's space. Fry until golden, turning over as each side cooks. It will
take about 10 minutes.

If you are serving them in the sauce you can leave them slightly pink in the middle at this
stage, but if you're eating them as they are, make sure they are cooked through but not dry.
To serve, cook the meatballs for another 15 minutes in the warm tomato sauce, then check for
seasoning and serve scattered with the fresh basil.

Chicken, apple and tarragon balls with sweet tomato salsa

These are definitely not your average meatballs. They started out as chicken and apple balls, finger food for my toddlers, but with a dusting of crumbs soon morphed closer to croquettes.

The kids loved them a little too much and every batch disappeared faster than I could make them, until I had my tarragon brainwave. Tarragon is fresh and lemony with soft, liquorice tones, but the aniseed factor is an acquired taste for kids, so it steers these little snacks into adult territory (until they cotton on, that is). They are incredibly useful for light lunches, piled up in small bowls with a sweet salsa on the side. **Feeds 4**

15 ml (1 Tbsp) chopped fresh tarragon
1 small eating apple, peeled, cored and finely grated
30 ml (2 Tbsp) full-fat Greek yoghurt
1 egg yolk
500 g minced chicken or chicken fillets chopped in a processor

1 pita bread, shredded into a small bowl and just covered in milk
Salt and freshly ground black pepper
1 egg, beaten
120 g croutons, finely blended in a food processor
Vegetable oil for frying

Mix the chopped tarragon, apple, yoghurt, egg yolk and chicken mince, then squeeze the milk out of the pita bread and add that too. Season well with salt and pepper. Roll into small walnut-sized balls and place on a baking tray lined with greaseproof paper. Cover with plastic wrap and chill for 20 minutes.

Take out of the fridge and roll each meatball, first in the beaten egg, then in the pulverised crouton crumbs.

Heat the oil in a large, heavy-bottomed frying pan and, when it's hot, add the balls in a spiral and fry until crispy and golden and cooked through.

Sweet tomato salsa
400 g cherry tomatoes, quartered
¼ red onion, very finely chopped
2.5 ml (½ tsp) crushed garlic
2.5 ml (½ tsp) finely chopped fresh green chilli

10 ml (2 tsp) finely chopped fresh coriander
5 ml (1 tsp) lime juice
10 ml (2 tsp) olive oil
Salt and freshly ground black pepper

Mix the tomatoes, onion, garlic and chilli together in a bowl. Add the coriander and stir through the salsa so it's evenly mixed.

Whisk the lime juice and olive oil together and season to taste with salt and pepper. Pour over the salsa and stir well. Leave for about 30 minutes to infuse, then serve with the meatballs.

Patties, cakes, fritters and other crunchy flat things

It's high time that patties, rostis and fritters step out into the spotlight. These 'crunchy flat things' are utterly delicious but, unfortunately, many cooks use them only as bases for loftier toppings. It might be because, badly done, they inevitably end up as greasy potato shreds that taste like cardboard, or soggy, mushy mouthfuls of unidentifiable roots. But, like many temperamental foodstuffs, it's worth persevering with a few recipes until you get things right.

Most savoury cakes are loosely formed and prone to disintegration, so start with a firm, well-shaped, even cake or a strong batter, and give it time to chill and relax for a while in the fridge. Next, make sure you have plenty of oil or butter in the pan, and fry or griddle them slowly. This will give you time to heat the patties through without burning them, until they turn golden, crispy and caramelised around the edges.

The truth is, if you treat them right, these salty, spicy, edible plates, stacked tall for main meals or bite-sized as starters with nothing more than spicy chutney for company are seriously tasty. If you can't face going down the fully vegetarian route just yet, head straight to the beginning of this chapter for the best ever veggie-loaded fishcake to get you started, and there will be no turning back.

No-stodge salmon and potato fish cakes with horseradish and watercress crème fraîche

Fish cakes drift off easily into claggy mounds if not treated with care, but these fluffy, crunchy, proper-sized patties are light, herby and perfect for lunch, especially when served with an icily hot horseradish crème fraîche and a bowl of crunchy green beans.

The key is to get the right consistency, so I like to dice the flesh tartare-style, and use bashed rather than mashed potato for bulk, before adding plenty of colour and texture with greenery. Once you've shaped the cakes, croutons pulverised in a processor give a crunchy, even coating, which sticks well to the fish and potato. You can make these ahead of time too – just pop them in the fridge for a couple of hours if you want the mess out of the way, then cook quickly before serving. **Feeds 4**

300 g potatoes peeled, cut into chunks.
60 ml (4 Tbsp) olive oil
2 cloves garlic, crushed
1 medium-sized red onion, finely chopped
60 ml (4 Tbsp) finely chopped fresh chives
90 ml (6 Tbsp) finely chopped watercress
Finely grated zest of 1 lemon

Salt and freshly ground black pepper
450 g salmon fillet, skinless, pin boned and
   finely diced
1 egg yolk
45 ml (3 Tbsp) cake flour
100 g finely blitzed croutons
Green beans, cooked, for serving

Boil the potatoes for 10–12 minutes until cooked but still firm. Mash half-heartedly, so that they're still a little lumpy, and then allow to cool.

Heat 30 ml (2 Tbsp) of the olive oil in a pan, add the garlic and onion and cook for 5 minutes. Remove from the heat and stir in the chives, watercress, lemon zest and a generous helping of salt and pepper. Mix well before adding to the mashed potato.

Add the diced salmon and egg yolk and gently stir through until you have a lumpy cohesive mixture. Using floured hands, shape into eight cakes and place on a floured plate.

Sprinkle the crouton crumbs onto a floured surface and roll the fish cakes over them several times until they are completely covered. Cover with plastic wrap and chill in the fridge for about 30 minutes.

While the fish cakes are resting, make the horseradish and watercress crème fraîche.

Heat the remaining 30 ml (2 Tbsp) oil and fry the fish cakes carefully until cooked through, which should only take 4–5 minutes each side. Serve with the horseradish and watercress crème fraîche and green beans.

Horseradish and watercress crème fraîche

30 ml (2 Tbsp) creamed horseradish

100 ml crème fraîche

15 ml (1 Tbsp) finely chopped watercress

Salt and freshly ground black pepper

Mix the horseradish into the crème fraîche until smooth and creamy. Fold in the watercress and season to taste.

Chickpea, herb and lemon burgers with Peppadew salsa

Like my vegetarian friends, I'd been on the hunt for a decent veggie burger for years – one that wasn't dry, tasteless or prone to falling off the fork before it reached your mouth. The answer is to add pulses, in this case chickpeas, for density and bulk, and mix with mashed potato to bind it together, adding lots of fresh herbs for flavour. Serve with this zingy Peppadew® salsa and you'll have the best burgers in town. If you like goats' cheese, a slice or two on top is sublime. **Feeds 4–6**

2 x 400 g tins chickpeas, drained
400 g chunky mashed potato, mashed with 5 ml
  (1 tsp) butter but still a little lumpy
Finely grated zest and juice of 2 lemons
100 g Parmesan cheese, grated
1 egg, beaten
2 handfuls fresh flat-leaf parsley, leaves only,
  finely chopped
1 handful fresh chives, finely chopped
100 g cream cheese (with herbs and garlic if you
  can find it)

Good pinch of cayenne pepper
Salt and freshly ground black pepper
30 ml (2 Tbsp) olive oil for frying
2 cloves garlic, crushed
1 large leek, halved, finely sliced then chopped
30 ml (2 Tbsp) butter
2 x 100 g logs goats' cheese, sliced into
  5 pieces each

Break down the chickpeas in a food processor until they are smashed but still have a little texture. If you don't have a food processor, use a potato masher and a strong arm. Add the mashed potato, lemon zest and juice, Parmesan, egg, herbs, cream cheese and cayenne pepper. Season generously with salt and pepper and mix well.

Warm the oil and fry the garlic and leek until translucent but not browned. Add to the chickpea mixture and stir well.

Flour your hands and shape the mixture into 10 burger-sized patties and set on a floured baking tray. Cover with plastic wrap and refrigerate for 1 hour or overnight.

To cook the patties, heat the butter in a large frying pan and, when it's hot, add the patties, two at a time. Try not to move them too much or they will get crumbly around the edges. When the patties are nice and brown (probably about 5 minutes), flip them over and cook the other side. Cook the rest, adding more butter along the way if you need it.

If you're going for the goats' cheese option, lay a slice on top now and slide under a hot grill until melted and bubbling.

Serve hot, with a tangy mound of Peppadew® salsa to keep things lively.

Peppadew® salsa

¼ x 400 g jar medium or hot Peppadews®,
  drained
20 red cherry tomatoes
½ red onion, finely chopped

30 ml (2 Tbsp) chopped fresh chives
5 ml (1 tsp) white wine vinegar
90 ml (6 Tbsp) olive oil
Salt and freshly ground black pepper

Chop each peppadew into quarters. Halve or quarter the tomatoes if they are large. Mix the
Peppadews®, tomatoes, onion and chives together gently. Whisk the oil and vinegar together
and season to taste, then pour over the salsa. Eat on the day.

Courgette fritters that don't taste like old sponges

You either love or hate courgette fritters. Cooked carelessly, they're like eating a bath sponge, but on form they are bubbly, summery and utterly delicious. It's down to selection and timing. Choose your vegetable wisely and don't be tempted to use up some gnarly marrow that is past its prime – stick to the fresh young things with firm, bright green skins and barely formed seeds.

Like many vegetables with a high water content, you also need to drain your courgettes well otherwise you'll have a soggy mess, and don't hold back on seasoning or friends like onion and garlic because courgettes need help to shine. This isn't a good one to make ahead, though. Shorten the time from pan to plate and you'll be rewarded with bouncy, frisky, tasty little fritters. **Feeds 4–6**

500 g courgettes
5 ml (1 tsp) salt
200 ml plain Greek yoghurt
1 handful fresh mint leaves, finely chopped
Salt and freshly ground black pepper
40 g butter
60 g finely chopped onion

2 cloves garlic, crushed
30 ml (2 Tbsp) chopped fresh coriander
Zest of 1 lemon
3 eggs, beaten
100 g feta cheese, crumbled
50 g cake flour
45–60 ml (3–4 Tbsp) olive oil for frying

Grate the courgettes and toss with the salt. Place in a colander to sweat out the excess liquid, turning every now and then for 15 minutes.

Make the sauce by mixing the yoghurt and mint together, then season with salt and pepper. Set aside.

Melt the butter and fry the onion and garlic until soft. Set aside until cool.

Mix the coriander, lemon zest, eggs, feta and flour together. Season well. Stir in the cooled onion and garlic. Squeeze the courgettes to remove excess water, then add to the onion mixture.

Heat 15 ml (1 Tbsp) of oil in a frying pan and check that it's hot by dropping in a little bread. If it sizzles, it's ready. Cook the fritters in batches by dropping tablespoons of mixture spaced apart into the frying pan. Flatten each dollop lightly with a spoon and cook for 2–3 minutes on each side until golden brown. Repeat with the rest of the batter, adding more olive oil as necessary. Drain them on kitchen paper.

Serve with the yoghurt and mint sauce and eat quickly to avoid the old sponge problem.

Thai sweetcorn and spring onion fritters

This is one of my simplest recipes. Even though the fritters are full of different flavours, they are unbelievably easy to prepare. Eat them as a snack, like hot chips, piled high and piping hot straight from the pan, or as a starter served with plain yoghurt and sweet chill sauce on the side.

Try to make the batter a few hours in advance as it likes hanging around for a while before cooking. It's a very forgiving dish, so you can also play around with different herbs or swop the onions for other vegetables such as leeks or spinach When you're ready to eat, the fritters take minutes to cook but taste fabulous.

Feeds 4 as a starter

1 x 440 g tin sweetcorn kernels, drained
45 ml (3 Tbsp) finely chopped spring onions
2 cloves garlic, crushed
5 ml (1 tsp) ground coriander
5 ml (1 tsp) finely chopped fresh red chilli
30 ml (2 Tbsp) chopped fresh coriander, plus extra for serving
30 ml (2 Tbsp) cake flour
5 ml (1 tsp) baking powder
1 egg, beaten
Salt and freshly ground black pepper
Sunflower oil for frying

Place the sweetcorn into a bowl and mash it gently just so the kernels break up a little. Mix in all the other ingredients, except the sunflower oil, seasoning to taste. It won't be very wet and you might think it doesn't have enough liquid, but it does.

Heat 15 ml (1 Tbsp) oil in a frying pan and swirl it around. When it is hot, drop dessertspoon measures of the mixture into the pan and flatten very gently. Don't allow the fritters to touch. Fry for 3–4 minutes until the underside is golden, then gently flip over and cook the other side.

Serve hot, scattered with more chopped fresh coriander.

Carrot, parsnip and cumin rosti

Oh, I do love a rosti! It is so much more interesting than toast or fried potato as a base, just as crispy, and waiting to be piled high with interesting treats. Rough rostis are greasy and chewy but here the grated vegetables caramelise and weld themselves together into rosti radiance, crisp and golden on the edges, yet meltingly soft inside.

This recipe uses winter root vegetables to make a sweet foundation that is tempered with flecks of nutty, lemony cumin to make earthy, substantial and colourful fritters. Great as a side dish with grilled meat and fish, or for lunch with a simple side salad and a dollop of chutney. **Feeds 4–6**

400 g potatoes, peeled and halved
250 g carrots, peeled and halved lengthways
250 g parsnips, peeled and halved lengthways
30 ml (2 Tbsp) salted butter
3 medium shallots, finely chopped
5 ml (1 tsp) cumin seeds, crushed
5 ml (1 tsp) ground cumin
1 egg
30 ml (2 Tbsp) chopped fresh parsley
Salt and freshly ground black pepper
45 ml (3 Tbsp) cake flour
Butter for frying

Bring a large saucepan of salted water to the boil, and add the potatoes, carrots and parsnips. Parboil for 12–15 minutes until tender but not soft or crumbly. Drain and leave to cool.

Heat the 30 ml (2 Tbsp) butter in a pan and gently fry the shallots for 4 minutes. Add the cumin seeds and ground cumin and fry for another minute. Set aside to cool.

Beat the egg in a large bowl, add the parsley and season with salt and pepper. Coarsely grate the cooked potatoes, carrots and parsnips into the bowl, then add the cooled shallots and mix. Sprinkle over the flour, stir and season well.

Heat a knob of butter in a frying pan and, when hot, drop in large spoonfuls of the rosti mixture, leaving spaces between them. Flatten gently and tidy the edges with the back of a spoon. Cook for 5–6 minutes before turning over. The rosti should be cooked through and golden on each side but not burnt. Remove and keep warm, then add a little more butter and mixture and repeat the process until the mixture is finished.

Serve hot with a sweet chutney.

Olive and pesto swirls

These funky little swirls aren't main meals, but they are excellent for a quick snack at parties. They are like savoury forms of the Labyrinth biscuits you'll find in the sweetness chapter (see page 172), but are a darn sight easier to make. You can use most savoury pastes, though here I've stuck to tapenade and pesto. Strong colours work well, especially pesto, as its brash green turns into a beautifully muted olive colour when cooked. As long as the pesto is concentrated and salty enough to balance the bluff wall of puff pastry, it will taste great. **Makes 20–30**

1 x 400 g roll ready-made butter puff pastry
Flour for dusting
45 ml (3 Tbsp) tapenade (you can also use other savoury pastes like anchovy or sun-dried tomato)
45 ml (3 Tbsp) pesto
Salt and freshly ground black pepper

Lay out the sheet of puff pastry on a lightly floured surface and dust with a little flour. Using a floured rolling pin, roll out to add another third to the overall rectangular shape. Trim the edges so that they are perfectly straight and cut the sheet in half (across the width).

Spread 45 ml (3 Tbsp) tapenade over one half and 45 ml (3 Tbsp) pesto over the other. Season well. Roll them up separately like two Swiss rolls and wrap in plastic wrap to firm up, without squashing them or losing their shape. Chill in the fridge for 1 hour or more.

Heat the oven to 200 °C.

Remove the pastry rolls from the fridge and trim the ends off each roll without applying too much pressure. Cut into thin medallions.

Lay the swirls on a baking tray with space in between and bake in the oven for 8–10 minutes until golden.

Eat as soon as they are cooked – they won't thank you if they have to hang around.

Better outdoors:
picnics and braais

There is an old saying that men, children and animals are all better outdoors. I'm not sure about men, but I'd certainly add food to that list. There is something magical about eating alfresco, whether it's watching the sunrise with a bacon roll, toasting marshmallows under starry skies, or sharing a glass of ice-cold wine with friends in the garden. What can be mundane in the kitchen quickly becomes sprinkled with fairy dust when you take it outside.

It doesn't have to be summertime, either. Chewing the fat over smoky food after a stressy week is my guaranteed fast-track route to relaxation, so unless there's a howling gale I'll even braai in a garage, because warming your hands by the fire is still way more fun than huddling around a stove in the kitchen.

When open-air meals are impromptu, being without your kitchen can also be liberating. Being outdoors has a habit of making everyday food rise above the ordinary and your guests obligingly more appreciative. The simplest ingredients come into their own when you have to make do, like baked potatoes which never taste better than when they're wrapped in foil and poked out of a campfire with a stick, skins blackened and white flesh scalding hot and fluffy inside.

If you aren't well equipped for the adventure, foraging for local goodies and cooking equipment only adds to the fun. Our favourite risotto was made from lime green seaweed picked off the rocks at low tide, and an old banana bread recipe turned out a cake worthy of the best patisserie when we baked it in empty tins during a weekend in the bush.

But if you do have the luxury of time, do a little prep in advance and you can eat smart food in the middle of nowhere. Before you leave the house, peel and bag veggies, and make salad dressings and marinades to pack in jam jars. Some dishes, especially those in marinades, will thank you for the ride and even benefit from a bit of jiggling around in the back of the car.

Eating outdoors turns any gathering into an event, because crossing the threshold between inside and out seems to infuse everyone with holiday spirit and a sense of occasion. The fresh air helps but it's also about logistics and freedom from formality. Outside, mess is irrelevant, and manners don't matter, as long as you have space to run around, breathe and live. Eat with your fingers, use a leaf for a plate, boil pasta with clean seawater, sit the dog in a chair, do whatever makes you smile, because normal rules and boundaries don't apply once you're through the door.

Sweet and saucy prawn and sesame sticks

This is roll your sleeves up and get messy food, ideal as an icebreaker for tricky guests, the in-laws, or when you need a leveller to get the party started. Prawns are ideal braai food, but they do require your full attention. It's best to treat them as the stroppy treat food they are, expensive and demanding on time and pocket, but worth it for the subtle flavours they absorb into their velvety flesh.

The marinade will coat around 25 large prawns with a sticky, delicious syrup, and because they don't require much cooking, there's less chance of the marinade burning. They are best braaied with the shells on to prevent the meat from drying out, and the trick to stopping them from turning rubbery or even worse, powdery, is to be a helicopter parent, hovering over the flames ready to snatch and serve them up, hot and fragrant onto the nearest plate.

The marinade keeps in the fridge for up to a week, so if you're going away for a weekend somewhere remote, take it with you in a jam jar. **Feeds 4–6**

25 ml (5 tsp) sesame seeds
25 ml (5 tsp) sesame oil
30 ml (2 Tbsp) crushed garlic
30 ml (2 Tbsp) soy sauce
25 ml (5 tsp) mirin (rice wine)
25 large king prawns, shell on

Mix all the ingredients, except the prawns, together in a screw-top jar. Shake well.

In a large flat dish, 3 hours (or a minimum of 45 minutes) before cooking, pour the marinade over the prawns and turn over to coat evenly.

Leave them in the mixture until you are ready to cook, then make your kebabs, or spike the prawns evenly onto your metal or presoaked wood skewers.

Braai carefully and evenly over medium coals until cooked – about 3 minutes each side. If there is a lot of marinade left in the dish, pour it over the prawns as they cook, being careful to avoid splashes and sizzles.

Leave on the skewers and serve immediately with just a few spoonfuls of gentle Jasmine rice salad (see page 89) to keep things cool.

Lightweight's chicken with coriander-flecked marinade

If big steaks and hefty burgers aren't your favourite thing, this may be the answer. It started out life as a skinny feast for a marathon running friend before the big race, but I've never served it up since without someone asking for the recipe.

So many low-fat marinades are bland and tasteless, using complicated chemicals to create flavour, but here you'll find none of that, and no oil or sugar either, just plain yoghurt and spices in a clean, summery marinade speckled with coriander. Best of all, you can make it the day before you cook, and unlike some marinades that leave you with nothing but old leather to chew on, the yoghurt and nuts in my skinny version help keep the chicken moist and tasty. If you're cooking for those with nut allergies, you can leave them out as it still tastes great. **Feeds 4 as part of a braai**

150 ml (10 Tbsp) natural yoghurt
5 ml (1 tsp) ground cumin
5 ml (1 tsp) ground coriander
2 cloves garlic, crushed
5 cm piece fresh ginger, peeled and finely grated
2.5–5 ml (½–1 tsp) deseeded and finely chopped green chilli, depending on your chilli tolerance
15 ml (1 Tbsp) lime juice
30 ml (2 Tbsp) ground almonds
2 large handfuls fresh coriander, stalks removed, finely chopped
8 free-range chicken thighs and drumsticks, skin on, bone in
2 limes, quartered

Mix the yoghurt, cumin, ground coriander, garlic, ginger, chilli, lime juice, almonds (if using) and fresh coriander together in a big bowl. Add the chicken and turn over in the marinade so it's all well coated. Cover with plastic wrap and chill in the fridge for at least 4 hours, or overnight.

That's it. When you're ready to eat, cook the chicken pieces over a gentle, even heat for about 30 minutes until cooked through.

Serve with quarters of lime, a simple green salad and baked potatoes.

Bacon-crossed lamb burgers with rosemary and mint

Although beef is the traditional mince for homemade burgers, it can make for dry and crumbly patties, particularly if they are cooked for too long, which is easy to do. So a good alternative to beef is lamb mince, which doesn't just make fab, moist meatballs, it also makes excellent burgers, especially if you are happy to leave them a little pink in the centre.

My favourite trick for keeping burgers moist is to wrap them in two rashers of streaky bacon so that they look like meaty hot cross buns. It's quite a loose mixture so the bacon also does a great job of holding the mince together, and if you cook them in a hand-held double-sided grill, you can ensure they keep their shape. **Makes 6–8 good-sized burgers**

150 g fresh breadcrumbs
15 ml (1 Tbsp) very finely chopped fresh rosemary
30 ml (2 Tbsp) finely chopped fresh mint
4 spring onions, finely chopped
Zest and juice of 1 lemon
2 cloves garlic, crushed
1 egg, beaten
Salt and freshly ground black pepper
700 g minced lamb
12–16 rashers streaky bacon

Mix the breadcrumbs, herbs, spring onions, lemon zest and juice, garlic, egg and seasoning together in a large bowl. Add the mince and stir thoroughly. Form the mixture into 6–8 fat, equal-sized burger patties before wrapping each one in a streaky bacon cross.

Cook over medium coals for 4–6 minutes each side. Braai very carefully, taking care not to let the bacon fall off.

Serve on *roosterbrood* rolls (see page 14) or burger buns with the tangiest, sloppiest condiments you can find. If you need more carbs, the Mediterranean potato salad (see page 86) goes startlingly well with these.

Butternut medallions with honey, red chilli and sage

The compact flesh and natural sweetness of butternut squash make it tasty and robust enough to roast, mash or fry, but I prefer to make these sweet and spicy coins which cook quickly and give you a thick, satisfying round to bite into. Using a simple honey marinade to help them caramelise beautifully around the edges, they make a great first course with a little chutney, or with flame-seared meat from the braai. In winter, serve as a spicy, bright orange veggie side dish to cheer up pale Sunday lunches.

If you are feeling lazy you might be able to find the slices peeled and pre-cut, but it's not so hard to make your own. Choose a butternut with a wide neck, peel, then thickly slice into medallions, saving the rest of the butternut for making cannelloni (Smug oven bakes chapter, see page 110). **Feeds 4 as part of a braai**

5 ml (1 tsp) honey
5 ml (1 tsp) finely chopped red chilli
30 ml (2 Tbsp) olive oil
1 handful fresh sage leaves, ripped into small pieces
2.5 ml (½ tsp) crushed garlic
20 butternut medallions

Heat the oven to 200 °C or get the braai fire to medium–hot.

Mix the honey, chilli, olive oil, sage and garlic together and pour over the butternut medallions, turning them over so that they are well coated.

If you are braaing, put the medallions on a grill over medium–hot coals, towards the edge of the heat, and turn frequently until cooked through, basting with the marinade as you do so.

If the butternut medallions are going into the oven, lay them on a greased baking tray and roast at 200 °C for 20 minutes, turning halfway through until they are golden and slightly caramelised around the edges.

Mediterranean potato salad with red onion, gherkin and herbs

Potato salads are the backbone of any self-respecting outdoor meal, bringing light relief and substance to meaty line-ups. This chunky, salty Mediterranean salad is absolutely the best so be warned, you'll need to make lots as it will disappear fast. Even those who think they hate gherkins, will love it; the gherkins contribute a satisfying crunch and a sharp bite that isn't vinegary at all.

The salad keeps brilliantly without collapsing, so you can keep sneaking back to the fridge for just one more spoonful. All of which makes this a zesty fighting salad rather than those cloying mayonnaise-heavy pot luck supper favourites. Make a few hours ahead and cover with plastic wrap for the best results. **Feeds 4 as part of a braai**

1 kg waxy new potatoes
6 small gherkins, drained and finely chopped
1 small red onion, halved and very thinly sliced, like wafers of onion rather than slices
1 large handful fresh dill leaves, finely chopped
30 ml (2 Tbsp) finely chopped fresh parsley
90 ml (6 Tbsp) of mayonnaise or salad cream/French mayonnaise
5 ml (1 tsp) lemon juice

Bring the potatoes to the boil in a big saucepan of salted water. Let them boil until they are cooked but not mushy, 10–15 minutes depending on their size.

Meanwhile loosely mix together all the other ingredients in a big bowl.

Rinse the cooked potatoes in cold water and allow to cool before gently peeling the skin off with your fingers. Slice the potatoes horizontally so they become two flat discs. Chop into big, uneven chunks and toss carefully in the dressing without breaking.

Jasmine rice salad with petits pois and fresh dill

When friends and family arrive for a party or braai, rather than doing the martyr thing over a hot stove, get cracking on this mild rice salad in advance and you too, shall go to the ball.

Rice salads can be crunchy, brittle affairs, poor relations to potato or pasta salads, but here the rice is mixed with bright green herbs and peas, which keep it light and add colour, sweetness and body. Use petits pois, which are tiny and even sweeter than standard peas. They don't need cooking, just defrosting with boiling water to stop them becoming dry and chewy. Serve at room temperature. **Feeds 4 as part of a braai**

250 g jasmine rice
15 ml (1 Tbsp) olive oil, plus extra for drizzling
2 small shallots, finely chopped
150 g petits pois
15 ml (1 Tbsp) finely chopped fresh parsley
2 large handfuls fresh dill, feathery leaves only, finely chopped, plus an extra handful to scatter
**   artfully over the top**
Salt and freshly ground black pepper

Rinse and cook the rice according to the packet instructions. While it simmers away, heat the olive oil in a small frying pan and gently sauté the shallots until transparent. Remove from the heat and scatter them in a wide, shallow serving dish.

Place the frozen peas in a colander and run boiling water over them a few times until they are defrosted. Add to the shallots and stir well, then bring on the chopped parsley and dill and stir that in too.

Drain the rice and stir it through the pea mixture, before seasoning and running through a little extra olive oil to separate the grains. Serve with extra dill scattered over the top, or allow to cool before covering.

Show-off's Caesar salad

A good Caesar salad should satisfy a humble check list before it is worthy of a main meal, namely, does it have: vigorous green leaves, a robust dressing, and golden, crunchy croutons? Doesn't sound difficult, but order one in a restaurant and they are invariably vile, made from watery, preservative-enhanced dressings out of a bottle (or worse, a packet), limp lettuce, and croutons that shatter your back teeth in seconds. Nasty.

I like to keep an open mind, but after yet another soggy lunchtime horror I had to create my own super-Caesar. You'll be so glad because this really is the best all-singing, all-dancing dressing ever. It will fill your heart with joy, set off your taste buds and leave you wondering why you've never made it before. The downside is that it will turn you into a terrible salad snob, because you, too, will have the secret to the best Caesar salad on the planet and won't be able to tolerate anything less.

Being a purist, I stick to cos lettuce leaves, Parmesan shavings and croutons, but if you need to add more protein it won't hurt to add extra anchovies, chicken or bacon on top of the finished salad. **Feeds 2 as a main meal, 4 as a light starter**

1 egg
4 anchovy fillets, drained and roughly chopped
10 ml (2 tsp) capers
10 ml (2 tsp) Worcestershire sauce
5 ml (1 tsp) Dijon mustard
1 clove garlic, crushed
15 ml (1 Tbsp) lemon juice
60 ml (4 Tbsp) finely grated Parmesan cheese
175 ml (yep, really) olive oil
Freshly ground black pepper
2 large cos lettuce, freshly washed and dried
Croutons
Parmesan shavings for scattering

Bring a saucepan of water to the boil, then add the egg and boil it for 4 minutes. Quickly plunge the egg into cold water, peel then place in the bowl of a mini blender.

Spoon in the capers, Worcestershire sauce, mustard, garlic, lemon juice and grated Parmesan. Add 100 ml of the olive oil and blitz until thick and emulsified. Slowly drizzle in the remaining oil, bit by bit. Season with black pepper and taste.

Place the lettuce leaves in a big bowl, pour over the dressing, mix well, then sprinkle with croutons and Parmesan shavings and serve immediately.

Supermarket trout ceviche

Ceviche tastes of the sea, summer and holidays. Dancing with flavour and life, this basic seafood dish from Peru is made from slices or chunks of raw fish, marinated in citrus juices, herbs and spices. The acid in the juice 'cooks' the fish and makes for a crisp, sharp starter or lunch.

Although it's traditionally made with white fish, my favourite ceviche was eaten on an hour-long touristy fishing trip. A shoal of mackerel miraculously caught on everyone's hand lines, and they were quickly hauled onboard, shimmering blue and silver, and filleted on deck. After a rinse with sea water we made a hasty ceviche, mixing the flesh with lemon juice, garlic and chilli in an old Tupperware. Ten minutes later we ate the whole lot, mopping up the juices with a loaf of bread as we bobbed up and down in the waves.

Sadly most of us are not often on boats, but this recipe can provide you with a taste teleportation to sea and summer after nothing more than a trip to the supermarket. This is for trout but you can also use salmon or most firm fish. **Feeds 4 as a light starter**

400 g trout or salmon fillet, skin removed
1 shallot, very finely sliced
Juice of 3 limes
Juice of 1 lemon
Juice of 1 orange
15 ml (1 Tbsp) olive oil
1 red chilli, finely chopped
2.5 ml (½ tsp) salt
Freshly ground black pepper
1 good handful fresh coriander leaves

Slice the trout as thinly as possible, and lay the slices in a small, shallow bowl.

Mix the shallot with the citrus juices, oil, chilli and salt and a little black pepper. Pour the marinade over the trout, cover and leave in a cool place or the fridge for 1 hour.

When you are ready to eat, serve with a sprinkle of coriander leaves and crusty bread.

Camembert and courgette heart tart

This is an unashamedly cunning cheat's pie that requires minimal effort and few ingredients to create a show stopper that will earn you stacks of brownie points.

Making food in different shapes can increase its impact dramatically, and here it gives a sense of grandeur that a simple puff pastry tart wouldn't otherwise deserve. Serve straight from the oven with a green salad and garlic bread. **Feeds 4**

1 x 400 g roll ready-made butter puff pastry
30 ml (2 Tbsp) olive oil
1 clove garlic, crushed
250 g small courgettes, thinly sliced
200 g Camembert cheese, cut into long, flat slices

4 big Italian plum tomatoes, stalks removed and
    thinly sliced lengthways
1 handful small fresh basil leaves
Salt and freshly ground black pepper

Preheat the oven to 200 °C.

Lightly flour a large baking sheet and unroll the puff pastry directly on top. Using a floured rolling pin, roll out the pastry by another 5 cm on each side, and gently cut out the biggest heart shape you can make. It shouldn't be longer than 30 cm from the bottom of the heart to the little 'V' in the neck. Set the trimmings aside.

Score a line (without going through the pastry) 3 cm from the outer edge, effectively making a heart within a heart. This empty area will rise during cooking and make a useful border to hold everything else in.

Heat the olive oil in a frying pan and, when hot, add the garlic and courgette slices and fry for a couple of minutes until slightly golden on each side. Set aside on kitchen paper to drain.

Back to the heart. You need to arrange diagonal rows of cheese and vegetables across the heart, so start at the top left (or right depending on your preference) and lay overlapping rows of courgettes, Camembert and tomato slices, tucking each one under the row before. Remember to leave open the border around the outside of the heart. Work down from your starting line to the bottom, tucking under as you go. When you are finished you should have a fabulous stripy effect across the heart.

Re-roll any trimmings and use to make shapes to decorate the heart. My family are used to seeing their names in pastry on my tarts and pies, but make whatever you fancy.

Rip the basil leaves and scatter half of them over the tart, then season with generous amounts of salt and pepper. Drizzle over a little olive oil or use the juice from the courgette pan and place in the oven for 25 minutes until the pastry is puffed and golden. Sprinkle with the rest of the ripped fresh basil and serve immediately.

Smug oven bakes
for time-poor cooks

Being relaxed and able to join the party makes for a happy cook, and my enduring love of one-pot dishes began with a light bulb moment, when I realised the best meals happened when supper was oven-ready before the doorbell rang.

Whatever you do, whether it's work, family or just lazing around in a trustafarian style (I wish!), there will be times when you can't cook. Perhaps the day was too manic, you just don't feel like it, or you'd rather be a guest than a red-faced skivvy stressing in the kitchen. Whatever the reason, that's when you'll be needing one of these smug oven bakes.

These are meals that bring us together too, as we gather to watch steam blast out of a golden chicken pie, or wait impatiently, teased by wafts of garlic from that rich beef stew that is somehow always ladled out too slowly.

Traditionally the one-dish or oven bake has been an informal affair, a kitchen supper or party favourite, but because it carries the weight of responsibility for the whole meal, it still needs to be good. That doesn't have to mean hours of preparation, as half of these recipes will still deliver depth and spectacle after a short cooking time. Everything here can be made ahead, ready to be delivered gorgeous and complicated-looking after a spell in the oven and a quick shout out to your guests.

No-brainer pot roast chicken with bacon, leeks and cider

This is a wonderfully friendly pot roast. It's so easy that everyone from the smallest to the grumpiest in the household can be the chef, and supper will still taste amazing. Basically you grab a handful of veggies, some bacon, and a chicken, then find a glass of cider, wine or chicken stock (if alcohol's not for you) and stick the lot into a big pot with a few herbs and a tight lid. Bake for a few hours, then eat. If that was too quick, here's the slow version. **Feeds a hungry foursome**

30 ml (2 Tbsp) olive oil
2 cloves garlic, crushed
1 red onion, chopped
2 rashers streaky bacon, snipped into small
   pieces
2 leeks, sliced into medallions
2 kg whole chicken
6 carrots, peeled and quartered
1 x 330 ml bottle cider or the same quantity
   white wine (If you prefer not to use alcohol,
   you can also use chicken or vegetable stock
   instead)

5 ml (1 tsp) dried thyme or 15 ml (1 Tbsp) fresh
   thyme leaves
Salt and freshly ground black pepper
60 ml (4 Tbsp) double cream
15 ml (1 Tbsp) wholegrain mustard
30 ml (2 Tbsp) finely chopped fresh parsley

Heat the oven to 180 °C.

Gently warm the olive oil in a stovetop-to-oven casserole, then add the garlic, onion, bacon and leeks. Cook on a medium heat, stirring continuously, until the leeks and onions are cooked but not brown.

Place the chicken in the casserole, breast side up, on top of the vegetables. Place the carrots snugly around the bird and pour over the cider or white wine. Sprinkle with thyme and season with salt and black pepper. Put on a tight-fitting lid and cook in the oven for 1 hour. Remove the lid, baste the chicken with the juices and return to the oven for 20–30 minutes until the breast side is golden brown.

Take the casserole out of the oven and check that the chicken is cooked through. Transfer the chicken and vegetables into a warm ovenproof serving dish, but leave the juices in the casserole. Cover the chicken with foil and return to the switched-off oven to keep warm.

On the stovetop, bring the juices to the boil in the casserole and reduce a little. Turn the heat down and add the cream and mustard, stirring without boiling until warmed through. Transfer the sauce to a warm jug, scatter the chopped parsley over the chicken and vegetables and serve immediately.

I love chicken pie

This is the ultimate cross-brood comfort food. Friends feel welcome, children are reassured by a tasty sauce happily free of suspicious green things, and oldsters come over all sentimental for days long past. A good chicken pie is a thing of beauty and I guarantee as you gaze on the honeyed golden crust, and watch the steam blasting out, filling the room with splendid wine, herb and garlic fumes, at least one of your guests will sigh and say 'I love chicken pie'.

Old-fashioned pies, particularly those made from Christmas leftovers, traditionally contain poultry and pork, in the form of remaindered turkey and diced gammon, but to make this work all year round, I use sausage meatballs. Not just tasty, they're a good excuse for kids to get messy by squeezing the meat out of the skins. Use super herby sausages if you want extra flavour as they will finish the pie off beautifully.

Puff pastry is my favourite freezer stand-by, and if you are seriously time poor, make the filling itself a few days before, and assemble at the last minute. It's a tradition in our house that everyone eating the pie gets their initial in pastry on top, another good job for the kids. Give them free rein and you'll get a masterpiece on top of yours.

Pie dishes come in many different shapes and sizes, and usually the older and more battered they are, the better they seem to cook. For this recipe, as long as the mixture reaches the top of the dish so that the pastry can sit snugly on top, the shape doesn't matter, but I usually use an old enamel baking tray which is about 20 x 25 cm and 4 cm deep. **Feeds 6–8**

30 ml (2 Tbsp) olive oil
30 ml (2 Tbsp) butter
2 cloves garlic, crushed
1 medium-sized red onion, finely sliced
1 leek, finely sliced
1.5 kg skinless, boneless chicken thighs, cut into four pieces each (or six if they are huge)

15 ml (1 Tbsp) chopped fresh parsley
7.5 ml (½ Tbsp) picked fresh thyme leaves, chopped
6 medium-sized carrots, peeled and sliced into coins
60 ml (4 Tbsp) cake flour
350 ml white wine
100 ml hot chicken stock
60 ml (4 Tbsp) fresh cream

15 ml (1 Tbsp) wholegrain mustard
Salt and freshly ground black pepper
6 fat, best-quality-you-can-afford pork sausages
1 x 400 g roll ready-made butter puff pastry
1 egg, beaten

Heat the oven to 200 °C.

In a big stovetop-to-oven casserole, heat the oil and butter gently, then add the garlic and onion and sauté gently until translucent. Add the leek, chicken, parsley, thyme and carrots and cook gently for 15 minutes until the chicken is lightly cooked but not boiled. Sprinkle over the flour and mix in thoroughly, then slowly add the white wine, followed by chicken stock.

Bring to a simmer and cook for 10–15 minutes, stirring frequently to reduce the sauce a little. Check that the chicken pieces are cooked through, then turn the heat right down and stir in the cream without allowing it to boil. Add the mustard and season to taste, then pour the mixture into your favourite pie dish (see introduction above) and set aside.

Cut the sausages from their string and (at this point, if there are kids around, call them over) squeeze out walnut-sized balls from each sausage skin to make about 30 little sausage meatballs.

Heat a nonstick frying pan and brown the sausage balls, then drop them evenly over the pie filling. Be scrupulously fair about distribution as it will save arguments later.

Roll out the pastry to the size of your pie dish, saving a little strip for decorations. If you have a pie bird or chimney, place it in the middle at this point. Drape the pastry over the dish and trim the edges, adding the trimmings to your decorating strip. Use a fork to make indentations all around the edges of the pastry and if you don't have a pie bird, cut a hole in the centre to allow the steam to escape when it bakes.

 Decorate the pie with pastry letters, hearts, whatever you feel like, then wash the pie with the beaten egg. Bake in the centre of the oven for 50–60 minutes, checking to see if it is golden brown on top before taking out.

This pie goes well with any carbs that have good mopping up qualities, but is, without doubt, at its absolute best with a pile of buttery, smooth mashed potato and a big bowl of peas.

Beautiful beefy stew with horseradish, thyme and parsley dumplings

This is a barnstormer of a stew with bags of flavour for family get togethers, celebrations, or just a quiet night in at club duvet. You can happily cook this in a *potjie*, but it comes into its own during the winter months, when nothing beats coming in shivering from the bleak cold to a soothing, comforting stew.

Savoury dumplings are quite dated because they used to be soggy balls of grey, semi-baked dough, but done properly they add a Seventies vibe and make an unusual alternative to mash, rice or couscous.

A couple of tips: Prepare the dumplings before you start the stew, making a firm dough and rolling the balls diligently into equal, meatball-sized dumplings with cool, floury hands. When the stew is made, fit the dumplings snugly on the top, sealing in the rich juices, and creating a crisp, pie-like topping. You can substitute wholegrain mustard for horseradish if you prefer. **Feeds 6**

Horseradish, thyme and parsley dumplings

75 g butter, frozen

150 g self-raising flour

15 ml (1 Tbsp) creamed horseradish or
   30 ml (2 Tbsp) wholegrain mustard

15 ml (1 Tbsp) fresh thyme leaves

15 ml (1 Tbsp) finely chopped fresh parsley

Salt and freshly ground black pepper

Coarsely grate the butter into a mixing bowl. Stir in all the other dumpling ingredients, season and mix together, adding 15–30 ml (1–2 Tbsp) water until you have a firm but malleable dough. Shape into meatball-sized dumplings, cover and refrigerate until needed.

Beautiful beefy stew

30 ml (2 Tbsp) olive oil

1 large red onion, sliced

2 cloves garlic, crushed

15 ml (1 Tbsp) chopped fresh thyme

45 ml (3 Tbsp) cake flour

2.5 ml (½ tsp) dried oregano

2.5 ml (½ tsp salt) and good sprinkling
   of freshly ground black pepper

1 kg diced beef or braising steak

6 carrots, peeled and quartered lengthways
   (halved if they are very large)

1 butternut squash (about 900 g), peeled and
   chopped into 5 cm cubes

400 ml easy-drinking red wine

400 ml beef stock

1 x 400 g tin chopped tomatoes

30 ml (2 Tbsp) tomato paste

To serve

1 clove garlic, crushed

Zest of 1 lemon

30 ml (2 Tbsp) chopped fresh parsley

Heat the oven to 160 °C.

Heat the oil in a large stovetop-to-oven casserole and gently fry the onion and garlic for
5 minutes, stirring frequently, then add the thyme.

While the onions are cooking, mix the flour with the oregano and season generously. Toss the
diced meat in the flour and mix until it's coated all over. Add the meat to the onions and stir.
Add the carrots, butternut, wine, stock, tinned tomatoes and tomato paste. Stir well so that it
is all pretty much covered by the liquid. Bring to the boil, cover with the lid and then place in
the preheated oven.

Cook for 2 hours. Taste and if the meat is still tough re-cover and place back in the oven for
another hour.

Mix the garlic, lemon zest and parsley with a pinch of salt and pepper, and stir into the stew.
Place the dumplings gently on top of the stew in concentric circles, keeping them close
together to form a tight-fitting, bubbly lid. Put back into the oven and cook, uncovered, for
20–30 minutes until golden. Serve straight from the casserole dish with tender broccoli or fine
green beans and don't plan on doing much afterwards.

Moroccan lamb shanks with spicy couscous

Lamb shanks can be strangely elusive so unless you have a friendly and resourceful butcher, I'd suggest you buy whenever they turn up and stick them into the freezer until needed. It's worth planning ahead, because this is an amazing dish. When you add the sweetness and heat of these Moroccan spices and a long, slow cooking session, they become impossibly tender and literally melt into the stew.

You can make this up to two days in advance and reheat thoroughly when you're ready. It takes a little preparation, but once you're done, just pop it into the oven and you can forget about supper for a while. This is a very rich dish, so although four adults might manage one each, one shank between two kids is enough.

Feeds 4–6

Lamb shanks

7.5 ml (½ Tbsp) cumin seeds

5 ml (1 tsp) coriander seeds

1 dried red chilli, crumbled and seeds removed
   if you like it mild

15 ml (1 Tbsp) cake flour

Salt and freshly ground black pepper

4 lamb shanks

30 ml (2 Tbsp) olive oil

3 cloves garlic, crushed

2 medium-sized onions, finely chopped

2 medium-sized carrots, finely chopped

3 sticks celery, finely chopped

5 ml (1 tsp) turmeric

2.5 ml (½ tsp) ground cinnamon

5 ml (1 tsp) sweet paprika

150 ml white wine

2 x 400 g tins chopped tomatoes, plus 1 tin
   refilled with water

15 ml (1 Tbsp) minced fresh ginger

30 ml (2 Tbsp) chopped fresh coriander

Heat the oven to 180 °C.

Crush the cumin seeds, coriander seeds and dried chilli using a pestle and mortar and mix with the flour. Season and roll the lamb in the flour mixture.

Heat the oil in a big stovetop-to-oven casserole and brown the lamb all over without burning. Take the shanks out and set aside.

Add the garlic, onions, carrots and celery to the casserole, put the lid on and cook them gently, stirring frequently for about 10 minutes until they soften. Add a little more oil if you need to. Stir in the turmeric, cinnamon and paprika and cook for about 2 minutes.

Add the white wine and let it simmer for 3–4 minutes with the lid off before adding the tinned tomatoes, water, ginger and finally, the browned shanks. Bring to the boil, cover and place in the oven for 2 hours.

Remove the lid and skim off any excess oil. Stir well and season to taste before returning the casserole to the oven for another 30 minutes. Before serving with the couscous, stir in the chopped fresh coriander.

Spicy couscous

5 ml (1 tsp) very finely grated lemon zest
¼ chargrilled red pepper from a jar (see page 115)
   or 3 sun-dried tomatoes in oil, chopped into
   1 cm pieces

¼ fresh red chilli, finely chopped
Salt and freshly ground black pepper
250 g couscous
250 ml (1 C) boiling water

Mix the lemon zest, red pepper and chilli with a little salt and pepper.

Cook the couscous according to the packet instructions or by placing it into a wide, shallow bowl, and just covering the grains with boiling water. Cover with plastic wrap and leave for 10 minutes or until the water has been absorbed. Take off the plastic wrap, sprinkle over the lemon and red pepper or sun-dried tomato mixture, and fork through the grains until the couscous is light and fluffy.

Statement spiral with peas, spinach and feta

Most traditional Greek cheese pies are round or triangular, but on the island of Skopelos, the filled pastry is curled into a spiral. Their pastries are normally stuffed with plain feta and herbs, but for a quick vegetarian main course, you can add substance and depth with my favourite veg, frozen peas. The result is a light and cool symphony in green, with gentle mint and dill to balance the feta's salty sharpness. **Feeds 4**

300 g fresh spinach
150 g frozen peas, defrosted
350 g feta cheese, crumbled
1 big handful fresh mint leaves, finely chopped
2 handfuls fresh dill, finely chopped, plus extra for serving

2 eggs, beaten but in separate bowls
Freshly ground black pepper
1 x 400 g roll ready-made butter puff pastry

Heat the oven to 200 °C.

Cook the spinach in a pan or microwave until soft and wilted. Drain, then chop finely before straining through a sieve, pushing on the spinach until no more liquid comes out.

Mix the spinach, peas, feta, mint and dill in a big bowl until well combined. Add 1 beaten egg and grind in black pepper to taste.

Cut the roll of puff pastry into four equal pieces and roll out a little bigger on a floured surface, so that you have four long rectangles.

Carefully place a quarter of the spinach and pea mixture in a line down the middle of each rectangle. Bring the two sides together and, using a little water on the edges to create a seal, overlap one edge on top of the other. Make sure the pastry doesn't break or the mixture will leak out during cooking. Do the same with the other pastry pieces so that you have four floury logs.

Line a baking tray with greaseproof paper and, starting from the centre, make a spiral out of the logs, making sure they fit snugly together. Brush lightly with the other beaten egg and place in the preheated oven. Bake for 25–35 minutes, and remove when golden.

Serve hot or cold sprinkled with extra chopped dill.

Butternut, sage and pine nut cannelloni

This is one of my favourite vegetarian meals, and I was delighted when my team of testers and helpers also voted this their favourite *Food for your Brood* recipe. Cannelloni is marginally more fiddly to make than lasagne, but the reward for extra effort is a beautifully tasty, tidy little pasta. Here, strong cheese and sweet tomato sauce bring a richness that brings the substantial filling to life, and as it handily uses a box of cannelloni, there'll be no stray rolls splintering into shards in the back of the cupboard for months afterwards. Try to make the filling, and cheese and tomato sauces in advance so that production is just an assembly job.

Feeds 6–8

Cheese sauce
60 g butter
60 g cake flour
900 ml milk

2.5 ml (½ tsp) prepared English mustard
150 g mature Cheddar cheese, grated
Salt and freshly ground black pepper

Melt the butter in a saucepan, then stir in the flour to make a tan-coloured paste. Add 15 ml (1 Tbsp) of the milk and blend, then add the rest, a little at a time, stirring constantly to remove lumps. Keep stirring until the sauce thickens and becomes glossy, then add the mustard and cheese and remove from the heat. Stir until the cheese has melted, then season with salt and pepper, cover and set aside.

Filling
1 kg butternut squash, peeled, diced into
  2 cm cubes
15 ml (1 Tbsp) olive oil
30 ml (2 Tbsp) chopped fresh sage

60 ml (4 Tbsp) grated Parmesan cheese
300 g drained ricotta cheese
50 g dry-toasted pine nuts
2.5 ml (½ tsp) salt
Freshly ground black pepper

Preheat the oven to 200 °C.

Pop the butternut into a roasting tin and mix in the olive oil, making sure the cubes are evenly coated. Bake for 30–45 minutes until soft and golden, then allow to cool. Bash the butternut into fluffy pieces (but not completely pulverised) and mix with the sage, Parmesan, ricotta and pine nuts. Season to taste (it will need a lot of salt), then spoon the filling into a plastic bag with the corner cut off and pipe it into the cannelloni tubes.

To assemble
12 cannelloni tubes
1 quantity Life-saving Tomato Sauce (see
  page 141)

200 g grated mozzarella cheese or 2 balls, thinly
  sliced

Heat the oven to 200 °C.

Pour the tomato sauce into an ovenproof dish and place the cannelloni tubes in the sauce, pressing down gently to submerge them slightly. Pour the cheese sauce over the top, making sure you completely cover the cannelloni tubes. Scatter evenly with mozzarella. Bake for 35–40 minutes until golden and bubbling and the cheese has melted.

Superfast ham, tomato and pesto lasagne

Who doesn't love this perfect Italian pie? It's the ultimate one-pot meal, with layers of meat, pasta and rich, creamy sauces melting together to make a wonderfully sloppy tower. I collect lasagne recipes the way spotters collect train numbers – avidly, greedily and with a beady eye for the unusual. Over the years I've been ruthlessly sorting my collection, endlessly fine-tuning to create my master list of perfect pasta bakes, a galaxy away from the stodgy, miserly offerings I always seem to end up with on aeroplanes.

The secret is to still make the lasagne as deep as you can, and layer generously with rich veins of sauce, pasta and cheese. In this version you'll find a suprise vein of pesto, which gives a basil kick halfway down. Make the tomato sauce in advance if you have time. **Feeds 4**

Tomato and basil sauce

45 ml (3 Tbsp) olive oil
2 cloves garlic, crushed
½ medium-sized onion, finely chopped
10 sheaves of basil, leaves removed and set aside, stalks removed and finely chopped
3 x 400 g tins chopped tomatoes
2.5 ml (½ tsp) sugar
Salt and freshly ground black pepper

Heat the oil in a saucepan, add the garlic, onion and basil stalks and cook gently until the onion is translucent. Add the tinned tomatoes, bring to the boil and then turn down to a simmer. Cook for 30–40 minutes until rich and syrupy. Add the sugar and season with salt and pepper to taste. Tear the basil leaves into small pieces and stir into the sauce.

Cheese sauce

50 g butter
40 g cake flour
700 ml milk
2.5 ml (½ tsp) Dijon mustard
100 g mature Cheddar cheese, grated
Salt and freshly ground black pepper

Heat the butter in a saucepan and, when it is melted, add the flour and stir well to make a tan-coloured paste. Without letting it burn, stir for a minute then add 15 ml (1 Tbsp) of the milk and mix in. Continue adding the milk, a little at a time and stirring constantly, until it is all incorporated without any lumps. Keep stirring over a low heat until it thickens and becomes glossy.

Add the mustard, and grated cheese, stirring while it dissolves in the sauce. Season with salt and pepper to taste, cover and set aside.

Lasagne

300 g fresh lasagne sheets
8 slices good-quality thick ham, ripped into small pieces
250 g ricotta cheese
45 ml (3 Tbsp) basil pesto
125 g mozzarella, sliced
1 handful fresh basil leaves for serving

Heat the oven to 180 °C.

Grease an ovenproof dish and pour in a third of the tomato sauce. Cover with a quarter of the cheese sauce, then a layer of fresh pasta. Scatter over half of the ham and ricotta, then add another layer of tomato sauce, cheese sauce and pasta.

Spread the pesto over the lasagne sheets, sprinkle over the remaining ham and ricotta, then add the last of the tomato sauce, a layer of cheese sauce and a final layer of pasta. Top with the remaining cheese sauce and cover with mozzarella. Bake for 50–60 minutes until golden brown. Serve scattered with torn basil.

Fiery pumpkin, sausage and hellfire veg traybake

When the nights turn dark and cold, keep your brood healthy and happy with this divinely easy traybake. Packed full of heat and colour, the combination of healthy veggies and tasty sausages helps to fend off autumn chills and winter flu faster than you can say antibiotic. It satisfies even the most stringent requirements of the one-pot supper, taking just a few minutes to prepare, requiring no effort to cook and being ready to serve straight from the oven 45 minutes later.

But don't feel you need to wait until someone's feeling peaky before you start peeling, as this works as a quick lunch or supper any time of year. You can also cover the roasting pan with plastic wrap and store it in the fridge for several hours before cooking. **Feeds 4 generously**

45–60 ml (3–4 Tbsp) olive oil
8 big fat sausages of your choice, preferably spicy
3 red onions, quartered
800 g peeled pumpkin, cut into big slices or chunks
2 chargrilled red peppers from a jar*, quartered (if you want to chargrill your own, see below)
5 cloves garlic, smashed, peeled and roughly chopped
½ fresh red chilli, chopped
1 handful fresh sage leaves, ripped into small pieces
Salt and freshly ground black pepper

Heat the oven to 200 °C.

Pour half the olive oil into a large roasting pan and swish it around to coat the base. Add the sausages, onions, pumpkin and red pepper quarters and pour over the rest of the oil. Turn everything over with a large spoon so that the ingredients are slickly coated with oil.

Sprinkle over the garlic, chilli and sage, add a good sprinkling of salt and black pepper and turn again. Roast for 35–45 minutes until the sausages are cooked, stirring well halfway through to make sure it's not sticking too much.

*If you can't find a jar of red peppers, prick 2 fresh ones with a knife and place in a preheated oven at 200 °C until the skin blisters and starts to turn black. Remove, place in a plastic bag and leave to cool. When they are cold, you will be able to peel them easily.

Sofa food for wintry nights

We all know how important it is to sit down and eat together as a family, but whether it's the end of term, a bad day or simply the arrival of a good friend, there are times when you just have to bypass the table and head determinedly for the sofa. But on the way, stop in the kitchen and make one of these sublime recipes, then you can put your feet up, cradle a bowl of beautiful sofa food in your lap and prepare to hunker down, secure in the knowledge that you need not move again for the rest of the evening.

There are a few rules for perfect sofa food, although they're more about logistics than regulations. Meals that can be eaten from a bowl avoid any of that slopping or sliding off the plate business and, ideally, you should be able to eat it with a fork or a spoon. Sawing steaks, extracting fillings or cracking crustaceans is fun, but usually best left to meals enjoyed around the table.

Cooking for the sofa is less demanding on the cook than flash meals because there's no particular need for beauty or spectacle, but the happiest memories still come from these simplest of times. Share your sofa food with the people you love or, even better, throw winter and a roaring fire into the mix, and as the weather lashes the world outside, you and yours can snuggle up, yummy food in hand, in heaven.

Frugal flash-fried teriyaki steak with sesame rice and broccoli

Fillet steak and frugal aren't words that normally go together but, strangely enough, when you're on a budget, that buttery richness comes in handy as you can get away with using small amounts.

This upmarket stir-fry marries beef fillet with an intense, sweet teriyaki sauce to create a flavoursome meal that satisfies without the need for big hunks of meat. Served with cool green broccoli and fragrant white rice, it needs little preparation, and even less cooking. Prepare the sauce and rice in advance and serve with a bowl of finely chopped red chillies to ramp up the heat. **Feeds 4**

120 ml homemade teriyaki sauce (see below)

2 cloves garlic, crushed

5 ml (1 tsp) grated fresh ginger

1 red chilli, seeds removed, very finely chopped

600 g fillet steak, sliced as thinly as you can, then
   cut into 2 cm wide strips

15 ml (1 Tbsp) sunflower oil

1 bunch spring onions, chopped

5 ml (1 tsp) sesame seeds

Steamed jasmine rice and broccoli for serving

Place the teriyaki, garlic, ginger and half of the red chilli into a medium-sized bowl. Add the beef strips, stirring and turning so they are well coated. Refrigerate for at least 20 minutes.

Heat the sunflower oil in a wok until very hot. Add half the beef and fry for 2 minutes, shaking the wok to brown the meat all over. Remove and keep warm. Cook the rest of the meat, adding more oil if needed. Return the warm fillet to the pan with the spring onions, stirring quickly.

Sprinkle the rice with sesame seeds, then serve with the fillet, broccoli and the remaining chilli on the side.

Homemade teriyaki sauce

Due to my family's noodle and sushi addiction we get through masses of soy and teriyaki sauce. Chinese supermarkets conveniently sell soy sauce in large vats, so that takes care of the sushi, but teriyaki is only available in small bottles, so I worked out how to make my own. **This makes about 250 ml (1 C) and will keep for up to two weeks in the fridge**

200 g castor sugar

120 ml (8 Tbsp) light soy sauce

60 ml (4 Tbsp) sake

10 ml (2 tsp) dark soy sauce

Warm the sugar and light soy sauce in a small saucepan, stirring all the time until the sugar has dissolved. Simmer gently for about 6 minutes until it thickens a little, then add the sake and dark soy sauce and let it cool before bottling.

It's all better now: prawn and ginger laksa

Laksas take comfort food to another dimension. The first taste sends your worries away in a steaming cloud of spicy coconut, along with your table manners, as the rest of the bowl will quickly have you slurping, munching and drinking like a demon.

It's all down to the laksa paste, a motley collection of hot, salty, sweet, cool and fragrant flavours that come together gloriously in a fiery taste rainbow. Simply add a tin of coconut milk and your chosen proteins and you've made the perfect laksa. It's easy, gorgeous and it **feeds 4.**

Laksa paste
You can buy sachets of paste, but homemade is oh, so much better. This makes enough paste for two meals and keeps in the fridge for a week, so you won't have to wait long between feasts.

4 handfuls fresh coriander, washed and split into
    leaves and stalks
45 ml (3 Tbsp) sunflower oil
4 cloves garlic, crushed
2 stalks lemongrass, outer leaves removed, very
    finely chopped
15 ml (1 Tbsp) grated fresh ginger

2 big red chillies, seeds removed, chopped
2 small shallots, chopped
5 ml (1 tsp) turmeric
6 lime leaves, stem removed and very finely
    chopped or crumbled if dried
30 ml (2 Tbsp) fish sauce

Roughly chop the coriander stalks (reserve the leaves for the soup) and place in a mini food processor with the rest of the ingredients. Blitz until very smooth.

Soup

120 g white rice noodles
45 ml (3 Tbsp) sunflower oil
60 ml (4 Tbsp) laksa paste (see above)
1 x 400 ml tin coconut milk
500 ml (2 C) chicken stock
2 handfuls pak choi (bok choy) leaves, chopped
30 ml (2 Tbsp) soy sauce

Salt and freshly ground black pepper
400 g raw prawns, shelled and deveined
1 red pepper, seeds removed and very thinly
    sliced
1 handful washed coriander leaves left over
    from making the laksa paste
2 limes, quartered

Pour boiling water over the noodles and soak for 12 minutes (or according to packet instructions). Drain and rinse in cold water. Set aside.

Heat the oil in a wok or big, shallow saucepan and fry the laksa paste for 3 minutes. Add the coconut milk and chicken stock, bring to a simmer and cook gently for 5 minutes. Stir in the pak choi and noodles and cook for 2 minutes.

Taste, add soy sauce and seasoning, then the prawns, and cook for 3–5 minutes until the prawns are cooked through. Divide into four bowls, sprinkle over the thinly sliced red pepper and coriander leaves and squeeze a quarter of lime over the top.

All-purpose pad Thai
with superspeedy peanut sauce

My mother was an early adopter of the stir-fry, and in those heady days of the oriental home food revolution, it was usually made with mince, vegetables and sherry and was utterly divine. We would happily have eaten it every day, except she was also experimenting with Indian and Turkish food, so stir-fries had to take their turns fairly, along with the rest of the world's cuisine.

My pad Thai brings a few more ingredients to the table but it shares the same stir-fry philosophy: bring together your favourite fresh foods, cook them quickly on the way to the sofa, have faith that it will taste amazing, and you won't be disappointed.

Peanut sauce is traditionally used as a dipping sauce for satay, but this one is light and pungent, packed with fresh herbs, and works beautifully drizzled over rice noodles. Make the sauce first as it keeps well for a few days in the fridge. **The pad Thai will feed 3–4**

Superspeedy peanut sauce

Peanut sauce is one of those universal sauces that you can use for dipping, marinating and noodling, as it works faultlessly every time. It's also one of the reasons I own a mini processor. Throw everything in, turn it on, scrape a bit and whizz again. How hard is that? Makes enough sauce for four meals unless you really, really love it, in which case, make that two

4 handfuls fresh coriander, stalks and all, washed and picked over to remove dodgy leaves
1–2.5 ml (¼–½ tsp) dried chilli or 1–2 fresh red chillies, roughly chopped
2 cloves garlic, crushed
Zest and juice of 1 lemon

30 ml (2 Tbsp) soy sauce
60 ml (4 Tbsp) crunchy peanut butter (try to use one that's not too sweet)
30 ml (2 Tbsp) water
Olive oil for covering

Stick all the ingredients, except the olive oil, into your trusty processor. Whizz for 1 minute, scrape down the sides with a spatula and whizz again and again until you have a smooth, soft paste that plops gently off a spoon. If it's too dry, add a bit more water. When it's ready, pour into a small dish and cover the top with a thin layer of olive oil to protect the colour.

Pad Thai

300 g wide, flat rice noodles

30 ml (2 Tbsp) fish sauce

2.5 ml (½ tsp) sugar

30 ml (2 Tbsp) soy sauce

½ fresh red chilli, finely chopped

60 ml (4 Tbsp) vegetable oil

4 cloves garlic, finely chopped

500 g boneless, skinless chicken thighs,
  cut into bite-sized pieces

1 red onion, thinly sliced

1 leek, halved lengthways and
  very finely sliced

2 eggs, beaten

80 g bean sprouts

2 spring onions, finely chopped

2 handfuls fresh coriander

4 lime wedges

30 ml (2 Tbsp) chopped roasted peanuts

Cook the noodles according to the packet instructions, drain, rinse and put to one side.

Mix the fish sauce, sugar, soy sauce and red chilli and set aside.

Heat 30 ml (2 Tbsp) of the oil in a wok, add the garlic, and stir for 1 minute. Add the chicken and fry quickly. Using a slotted spoon, remove and keep warm.

Pour the rest of the oil into the wok and add the red onion and leek. Fry for 3–4 minutes, then add the beaten eggs and cook quickly for a few seconds, scraping around the wok as you cook. Tip in the noodles, chicken and fish sauce mixture and heat through. Add the bean sprouts and cook until warm. Drizzle over 30 ml (2 Tbsp) of the peanut sauce.

Serve in warm bowls sprinkled with the chopped spring onions, fresh coriander, peanuts, lime wedges and extra peanut sauce on the side.

Pea and pig risotto with sparkling wine

For me, even the mere memory of my perfect meal can bring on an obsessive desire to eat it *now*. It was an encounter with risotto nirvana and it is sheer admiration, rather than an ulterior motive, that forces me to tell you where I found it.

On a Mother's Day lunch at Môreson in the Cape winelands, the chef, Neil Jewell, blasted a shaft of pure sunlight onto our table in the form of a sublimely creamy, dreamy risotto. It was so good we nearly left friendless thanks to a somewhat lively discussion with our fellow guests over who was taking the doggy bag home.

Sadly, I can't eat there every day, so rather than be risotto-less until the end of time, I reluctantly created a home cook's homage to his masterpiece. Although it's not as good as his, I reckon it's a pretty good substitute. The sparkling wine might sound over the top, but it brings an edge to counter the richness.

Feeds 2–4 for supper, or 4 for lunch as long as you're prepared to fight your corner

8 rashers streaky bacon or pancetta
1 litre (4 C) chicken or vegetable stock
40 g butter
15 ml (1 Tbsp) olive oil, plus extra for drizzling
1 clove garlic
1 medium-sized white onion, finely chopped
250 g risotto rice

250 ml (1 C) frozen peas (thaw quickly by
   pouring boiling water over them)
15 ml (1 Tbsp) sparkling wine
80 g Parmesan cheese, finely grated
Salt and freshly ground black pepper
15 ml (1 Tbsp) chopped fresh chives

Place the bacon or pancetta under a preheated grill and cook until crisp and golden. Cut into small pieces and keep warm.

Heat the stock in a small saucepan and keep warm.

Melt the butter and olive oil in a heavy-based saucepan and add the garlic and onion. Cook for about 5 minutes until translucent, then add the risotto rice and stir for 2 minutes until the grains are coated with the oil and butter mixture.

Add a ladle of the hot stock and stir until it has been absorbed by the rice, then continue adding stock a ladle at a time until it is finished. Don't add more until the previous ladle of stock has been absorbed by the rice. Don't rush, this will take a good 20 minutes, so get yourself someone to talk to. Taste the rice and, if needed, add more stock or water and keep stirring until it is absorbed. It should be firm to the bite, not flabby or crunchy.

Add the thawed peas and stir until warmed through. Make a space in the middle of the pan by pushing the rice to the side and add the sparkling wine, stirring until it has been absorbed.

Remove from the heat, stir in half of the Parmesan and season to taste. Sprinkle with the chopped, crispy bacon or pancetta, the rest of the Parmesan and the chopped chives. Drizzle with olive oil and serve with the ubiquitous fresh green salad.

Red onion, chorizo and cannellini bean pasta

Convincing kids to stray from their well-trodden pasta paths of bolognaise, pesto or macaroni cheese can be hard, but it's essential if you are to avoid a deadly dull family meal schedule. The best way to implement change is to ensure they don't have an option, which is how this spirited sauce came to be. It was born out of necessity, after a late-night homecoming meant the shops were closed, and a kitchen forage yielded only onions, a sad, dried up end of chorizo, tomatoes and a dusty tin of beans. No one was hopeful of a decent meal, but from those humble beginnings came a suprisingly feisty sauce with deep, dark flavours and a sly, spicy heat that has made it one of our favourites.

Cannellini beans have always been a store cupboard stand-by for dips and salads, but this recipe elevates them to the main feature. I prefer not to blend the sauce completely as a rustic texture works best, but do slice the onions as finely as you can. **Feeds 4**

30 ml (2 Tbsp) olive oil
150 g diced spicy chorizo
1 big red onion, halved and sliced as thinly as you can
3 cloves garlic, crushed
½ fresh red chilli, finely chopped or 1 ml (¼ tsp) dried chilli
2.5 ml (½ tsp) smoked paprika
2 x 400 g tins chopped tomatoes
7.5 ml (½ Tbsp) tomato paste
2.5 ml (½ tsp) sugar
7.5 ml (½ Tbsp) sherry vinegar
1 x 400 g tin cannellini beans, drained
Salt and freshly ground black pepper
500 g pasta of choice
Finely grated Parmesan cheese and 1 handful fresh basil leaves for serving

Heat the oil in a saucepan over a medium heat, add the chorizo and cook until golden. Turn the heat down and throw in the onion and garlic and stir until cooked but not brown. Add the chilli, paprika, tinned tomatoes, tomato paste and sugar and simmer gently for 25 minutes until rich and reduced.

Pour in the vinegar, stir for a couple of minutes and then add the beans. Keep cooking until they are warmed through. Season to taste.

Bring a pan of water to the boil, add 5 ml (1 tsp) salt and cook the pasta according to the packet instructions. Drain the pasta, stir in the sauce and serve in shallow bowls sprinkled with mountains of grated Parmesan and torn basil leaves.

Deconstructed basil pesto with linguine

I *love* pesto. Really, truly love it and from the moment it appeared on my radar it became my default comfort, night-in-on-the-sofa food. But it's a food of extremes. At one end of the scale was my friend Ned's pesto, made from annoyingly immaculate, raindrop-speckled, emerald green basil from his herb garden, whizzed up with top-quality olive oil and proper Italian Parmesan. In my fridge sat the complete opposite: jars of emergency pesto, a truly horrible, yellowy mess of stalks that tasted like grass.

Duly shamed, I created my own freeform, mixed media pesto that doesn't follow any pesto rules, but is so utterly delicious you could eat it straight off the spoon. Perfect for a party, no party or after a party. Just remember, pesto doesn't like to sit about, so make and eat it without any dithering. **This makes enough to feed 4**

6 handfuls fresh basil, gently rinsed, dried and leaves picked
2 cloves garlic, crushed
100 g good Parmesan cheese, finely grated
200 ml olive oil, plus extra for drizzling
30 ml (2 Tbsp) pine nuts
Salt and freshly ground black pepper
500 g dry linguine

Set aside a small handful of basil leaves, then place the rest into a mini food processor with the garlic, Parmesan and olive oil. Pulse for a few seconds, then use a spatula to scrape down the bowl. Keep pulsing until you have a rough, textured paste.

Add a little more olive oil if it's too stiff and pour into a small bowl. Taste and season with salt and pepper. Drizzle a little olive oil over the top just to keep the colour otherwise it will go brown very quickly.

That's the pesto made. Now dry-roast the pine nuts in a frying pan until they are golden brown all over. Be careful, I've thrown away a forest of these things because they burn the minute you turn your back. When the nuts are ready, save a teaspoon for serving, and pour the rest into the pesto, enjoying the spitty, hissy noises.

Bring a large saucepan of salted water to the boil and cook the linguine according to the packet instructions. Drain.

To serve, stir the pesto through the pasta, and tear the set-aside basil to scatter over the top. Sprinkle with the saved pine nuts for extra crunchiness.

Squodgy spinach gnocchi with sage butter

Homemade gnocchi is more work than opening a packet, granted, but it's so worth the effort. With just a little flour, the spinach and ricotta turns into goodness-filled, bouncy dumplings that need a mere sprinkling of Parmesan and a swirl of lemony sage butter to spark them into life. Make them once and you'll never buy mass-produced supermarket imposters again. **Feeds 4**

500 g baby spinach leaves, washed and dried
5 ml (1 tsp) butter
2 eggs
250 g ricotta cheese
Nutmeg
Salt and freshly ground black pepper
40 g Parmesan cheese, finely grated
60 ml (4 Tbsp) cake flour, plus extra for rolling

To serve
50 g butter
4 fresh sage leaves, shredded
40 g Parmesan cheese, finely grated

Pop the spinach and butter into a large pan over a medium heat. Stir until the spinach has wilted, then drain well and chop finely. Place in a colander and press with a potato masher to push out any excess water, then leave to drip while you prepare the dough.

Beat the eggs, then stir in the ricotta, a grating of nutmeg, some salt and pepper, the Parmesan cheese and the flour. Stir in the chopped spinach, cover and refrigerate for at least 2 hours.

Switch on the oven to about 50 °C to warm up, and bring a large saucepan of lightly salted water to the boil.

Scatter a little flour in a bowl, and on a plate. Remove the spinach mixture from the fridge and, using a dessertspoon, scoop a lump of the mixture about the size of a wine cork. Using another spoon to help, shape the dough into an egg shape. Drop into the bowl containing the flour and roll around so that it is lightly covered, then place onto the floured plate. The mixture is extremely sticky so it helps if you don't touch it with your fingers! Keep making the gnocchi, placing them on the floured plate when they are done, until all the mixture is used up.

Place the 50 g butter and shredded sage leaves into an ovenproof gratin dish and place in the warm oven to allow the butter to melt.

Turn the boiling water down to a simmer and gently drop in the gnocchi, about six at a time, using a slotted spoon. They will sink to the bottom, then rise to the surface when cooked, which should take 4–5 minutes. Remove the cooked gnocchi with the slotted spoon and gently place in a colander to drain, before transferring to the gratin dish. Sprinkle with a little Parmesan, turn gently in the melted sage butter and return to the oven.

Continue poaching the gnocchi in the simmering water, adding the batches of cooked gnocchi to the gratin dish each time they are cooked. To serve, remove from the oven and sprinkle with the remaining cheese.

Let them go:
food for fledglings

In an ideal world kids start out as happy eaters, and end up as healthy adults who don't eat too much or too little for their lifestyles. It doesn't sound hard, but the reality is that as a parent, you have a huge job to do, which starts with feeding them solids. At this point, you will occasionally be in control, but mostly, it goes like this: you mash, you offer, you scrape … off the ceiling/your hair/their face/the floor. If that goes well, the next stage is persuading them to eat the right foods, then persuading them not to eat the wrong foods, and so it goes on.

Although children can be fearful about new tastes, if you include them in the cooking process early, chances are they'll venture further outside their comfort zones when they are old enough to make choices. And apart from a little mess (okay, a lot of mess), it's all good. Babies love different sounds so start with button pressing, and the minute they can hold a spoon let them stir anything and everything. Then, with their interest piqued and fine motor skills increasing, it's time for you all to have some serious fun as you enter the icing-fuelled toddler years. As they grow up and start to get comfy in the kitchen, move on to create tasting opportunities for new and unusual food by teaching them to make it themselves. They might not go for the green stuff first time around, but I always find that if they make their own pesto they will soon be dipping a finger into it.

Kids don't need to be master chefs, but if they can cook a few basic dishes, everyone wins, from the tired parent surprised with supper to the teenager who gets to cook and be loved all the more for it. Once your fledglings leave home they will certainly be alone with a kitchen and a plate at some point, but if they can cook, they won't have to rely on micro-wavable gunk to fill it.

Food for fledglings is about infusing your children with a love of cooking and giving them the tools to feed themselves and their friends and family, as you do. Family recipes, infused with love, memories, stains and scribbles, pass through generations and are more trea-sured than most of our more tangible possessions. You will have to let your children go, but if you teach them how to cook, they will always have a direct line to home.

Stripy pasta

What is it about pasta machines that relegates them to hard-to-reach cupboards, to emerge only when it's time for a clear out? Mine sat forlornly in a friend's kitchen, dusty and unopened until she donated it to me, whereupon it lurked for months in my cupboard, until I was shamed into breaking the cycle.

I'm so glad I made the effort because this stripy pasta looks uber-complicated but is a breeze to make. Add the herb leaves to the dough before feeding it through the machine and watch in wonder as it weaves a beautiful minty green humbug stripe through the dough. **Makes enough pasta to feed 4–6**

500 g '000' or cake flour
5 eggs, beaten
5 ml (1 tsp) olive oil
1 handful fresh basil leaves

Put the flour into a bowl and make a well in the centre with walls high enough to contain the beaten eggs. Tip the eggs into the well and start mixing them, tipping over a little flour at a time into the well. It will be sticky, but keep mixing and eventually you will have a ball of dough.

Start kneading gently so that it becomes silky smooth and soft and pliable in your hands. If it really is too dry, add a few drops of the olive oil, but only if you need it.

Don't work the dough for too long – it shouldn't take more than 10 minutes. Once you're happy with the look of your little boulder, dust very lightly with flour, wrap in plastic wrap and leave to sit for 20 minutes.

Break off a lump of dough about the size of a small apricot, flatten it with your hand, and pass it through the widest grade on your pasta machine. Turn the cog so that it is slightly thinner and pass through again. Keep going until it's been through the machine five times.

If you want stripes (which, believe me, you do) lay out one sheet of pasta and place the basil leaves on top. Then place another sheet of pasta directly over the top and run both through the machine. You will see the leaves being pressed into the sheets. Run through a few times until the pasta has become stripy but doesn't tear easily.

Cut into long strips and leave to dry on baking paper or over coat hangers. It will only need a few minutes cooking.

Life-saving tomato sauce

This is a rich, crimson, big-hearted multitasker of a sauce that fills your kitchen with fabulous aromas and a warm, fuzzy feeling. It's hardy and versatile with no airs or graces, so go ahead and freeze, bake, boil or just eat it by the dreamy spoonful whilst you stand stirring at the stove.

Smooth it over pizza bases, mix with pasta for fast fuel stops, or wrap up a jar as a foodie gift for cheering up sad friends. And if you're home with a lousy cold, I recommend shuffling to the kitchen and filling up a soothing mugful to warm your hands and fill your belly. Add a pile of bread for dunking and everything will soon feel better. **Feeds 6 as a pasta sauce**

60 ml (4 Tbsp) olive oil
2 big cloves garlic, crushed
1 medium-sized red onion, finely chopped
1 carrot, peeled and finely diced
1 stick celery, finely diced
3 x 400 g tins whole tomatoes
2.5 ml (½ tsp) dried oregano or dried mixed herbs
Salt and freshly ground black pepper
5 ml (1 tsp) sugar
15 ml (1 Tbsp) chopped fresh basil

Heat the oil gently in a saucepan, add the garlic and onion and cook for 5 minutes to take the edge off. Add the diced carrot and celery, and cook gently without browning for 10 minutes. Pour in the tomatoes and dried herbs and stir. Bring to the boil slowly, then turn down the heat, partially cover and simmer very slowly for 35–45 minutes, stirring from time to time.

Taste and add salt and pepper, plus the sugar to add a hint of sweetness (some canned tomatoes can be slightly bitter). If the sauce is very thin, allow it to simmer for another 10 minutes until you have a chunky pouring consistency. Mash with a potato masher to break down the big pieces, rather than creating a fine purée. A coarser texture is my favourite, just without too many big veggie pieces. If your guests really don't do lumps, use a stick blender to create a smoother sauce.

Use immediately or allow to cool and freeze or store in the fridge for up to three days.

Party pot stickers

Pot stickers are literally little dumplings that stick to the pot. They are super tasty and quick to make, especially when you use ready-made wrappers and delegate production to the kids. You might find them fiddly but smaller, nimbler fingers cope with ease. When you're ready to go, set up a production line for your young guests and put your feet up. As soon as they get the hang of it, they'll be busy and competitive at their stations, churning out succinct little half-moon dumplings faster than you can catch them.

It's best to make a few fillings, using a base of different fresh herbs for each one. The fillings can be done the night before, covered with plastic wrap and refrigerated. The fussiest of kids or those who hate the green stuff will give these a try when they've been part of the production process. There were a few pulled faces at the spinach and cream cheese on our shoot, but they were the first to disappear at feeding time. You will need a large frying pan with a tight-fitting lid. **Each filling is enough for around 20 pot stickers**

Wonton wrappers (most oriental food shops sell them frozen, or you can get them online)
45–60 ml (3–4 Tbsp) vegetable oil for frying
135–180 ml boiling water or hot chicken stock
Cake flour for sprinkling

Pork, pak choi and chives filling

250 g minced pork
6 pak choi (bok choy) leaves, finely chopped
60 ml (4 Tbsp) finely chopped fresh chives
5 ml (1 tsp) crushed garlic
15 ml (1 Tbsp) finely chopped fresh ginger
5 ml (1 tsp) soy sauce
5 ml (1 tsp) sesame oil
Salt and freshly ground black pepper

Mix everything together, season well, cover with plastic wrap and refrigerate until needed.

Prawn, coriander and chilli filling

250 g shelled cooked prawns, chopped
20 g fresh coriander leaves, finely chopped
2 spring onions, finely chopped
5 ml (1 tsp) crushed garlic
5 ml (1 tsp) soy sauce
5 ml (1 tsp) fish sauce
5 ml (1 tsp) sesame oil
2.5 ml (½ tsp) finely chopped red chilli (optional)
Salt and freshly ground black pepper

Mix everything together, season well, cover with plastic wrap and refrigerate until needed.

Spinach and cream cheese filling

200 g fresh spinach
2.5 ml (½ tsp) sesame seeds (optional if you are frying)
5 ml (1 tsp) crushed garlic
1 x 230 g tub plain cream cheese
30 ml (2 Tbsp) soy sauce
5 ml (1 tsp) sesame oil

Cook the spinach, either in the microwave, or fry quickly with the sesame seeds, until wilted. Drain, then chop finely and strain through a sieve until it is dry.

Place the spinach and all the other ingredients in a bowl and stir well until it is completely blended. Cover with plastic wrap and refrigerate until needed.

Making the pot stickers
Sprinkle a little flour on a large plate or chopping board so that it is ready to receive the pot stickers.

Take a wonton wrapper and gently paint a thin line of water all around the edge with a pastry brush. This will help the edges to stick together.

Place 5–10 ml (1–2 tsp) of your chosen filling in the centre of the wrapper, then bring the two sides of the wrapper together, in a half-moon shape if the wrappers are circular or into a triangle if they are square. Gently press together until they are sealed. Carefully flatten the base of the dumpling so that it will sit upright in a frying pan or steamer. Repeat with each of the wrappers, setting aside the finished dumplings on a lightly floured surface.

When you are ready to cook, heat 15 ml (1 Tbsp) vegetable oil in a large frying pan, and carefully place about six dumplings in the pan, making sure they don't touch.

Fry for 3–4 minutes until the bottoms are golden and crisp, but not burnt. Add 45 ml (3 Tbsp) of boiling water or hot chicken stock to the pan. Don't be alarmed if it splutters, just quickly cover with a tight-fitting lid and leave them to steam for 3–5 minutes until all the liquid has been absorbed. Remove from the pan and keep warm. Repeat with the rest of the dumplings.

Serve hot with your favourite dipping sauce.

Smoked trout sushi balls
for squeamish kids

Getting your kids to eat sushi is a double-edged sword. On the one hand, you can be smug and happy in the knowledge that they are eating the healthiest food on the planet. On the other, sushi is addictive and eye-wateringly expensive. Those jolly little conveyor belts that dance around carrying oh-so-tiny platelets, are actually ruthless showcases for tasty morsels that kids find far too easy to inhale. When they get the taste for it, they will demolish mountains of plates in minutes, leaving a huge hole in your purse. Great that they want sushi above junk, but ouch, it costs, so best to make your own. That way, everyone's happy.

This recipe is a variation on basic nigiri, which is simply rice with fish or vegetables but the balls are easier to eat with fingers if the little darlings aren't chopstick wielding just yet. **Makes 20–30 sushi balls**

500 ml (2 C) raw sushi rice
85 ml rice vinegar
5 ml (1 tsp) salt
5 ml (1 tsp) castor sugar
100 g smoked trout, diced

10 cm length cucumber, chopped into 1-cm-long matchsticks
Soy sauce, preserved ginger and wasabi (optional) for serving
Black and white sesame seeds (optional)

Preparing sushi rice isn't difficult, but it does take time between stages. Rinse the rice thoroughly in a sieve. Use your hands to move it around to get out the starch out. It may take several washes, but when the water runs clear, drain and place the rice in a saucepan with the lid on. Leave to sit for 1 hour.

Add 500 ml (2 C) tap water to the pan and bring to the boil. As soon as it starts boiling, turn the heat down to a simmer and cover tightly. Simmer for 20 minutes, then don't take the lid off, just turn the heat off and let it sit for another 20 minutes.

While the rice is standing, mix the vinegar, salt and sugar together in a jug and stir until the sugar has dissolved.

Transfer the rice to a big, preferably plastic, mixing bowl. Pour the vinegar mixture over the rice and use a wooden spoon and chopping movements through the rice to cool it down. You want to cool it down by 'slicing' or chopping the rice, rather than turning it over as it keeps the grains intact and stops it becoming mushy.

When the rice has completely cooled, cover with a lid or place in a Tupperware. Sushi rice dries out quickly so it's good to keep it covered while you work.

Now, bring in the kids and give them each a bowl of water and a plate. Using wet hands, each child needs to make a ping pong ball-sized sphere of rice by rolling it gently around in their palms. When it is roughly the right shape, break it open and insert a few pieces of trout and cucumber. Remake the ball so that there is no filling showing. Continue until the rice is finished.

Serve with bowls of soy sauce and ginger, and wasabi for the more adventurous.

DIY pizzeria

Ask a random child what their perfect meal would consist of and pizza will probably be the answer. Mass produced hubcap-sized pizzas plastered in plastic cheese aren't ideal, but thankfully homemade pizzas are excellent, and hugely useful for encouraging kids to try out new ingredients.

A DIY pizzeria is also my default meal for big groups with too many opinions. The common denominator is tomato sauce and a pile of grated mozzarella, so lay those out alongside a bar full of toppings and seasonings, fire up the oven to its hottest setting and stand back and watch as the stampede begins. You'll be amazed at the creativity children will bring to the task – every time we make this, they up the ante, with the latest efforts including successful homemade stuffed crust margaritas. **Feeds 6**

500 g white bread flour
Good pinch of salt
1 x 10 g sachet instant yeast
30 ml (2 Tbsp) olive oil mixed with 375 ml (1½ C) tepid water in a jug
300 ml Life-saving Tomato Pasta Sauce (see page 141), or shop-bought pizza sauce
300 g mozzarella cheese, grated or sliced as you fancy
Topping suggestions: ham, salami, onions, basil, extra cheese, olives, mushrooms,
  olive oil, other cheeses
Freshly ground black pepper
Chopped fresh herbs
Olive oil for drizzing

Place the flour, salt and dried yeast in a big bowl and mix well. Make a well in the centre and gradually add the oil and water mixture whilst bringing in the flour from the sides, until it makes a soft, workable dough. Knead for about 10 minutes until it is soft, elastic and not too sticky. Place in a lightly greased bowl, cover with a clean tea towel/dishcloth and leave to rise until doubled in size.

Heat the oven to its highest setting and place a big baking or pizza tray inside.

Divide the dough into six and roll out, as thinly as you can, on a floured surface. Stack the rounds in a pile with a layer of baking paper between each one.

For each pizza, spread 30–45 ml (2–3 Tbsp) of the tomato sauce thinly over the base, sprinkle over grated mozzarella and scatter with toppings. If the kids want to make a stuffed crust pizza, they need to place a thin line of mozzarella about 1 cm from the edges of the dough, then roll the dough over the cheese to seal it in. Finish with a good grind of black pepper, fresh herbs and a drizzle of olive oil.

Let each kid make their own, and line them up. They will soon be fighting over whose goes into the oven first but don't worry, as they only take 10–12 minutes each.

Cool chicken quesadilla with sour cream and Peppadews®

Quesadillas are a kind of toasted sandwich made with wraps and they're a cinch for kids to cook themselves. All they need are a few ingredients, a little assembly time and a hot pan. If you have leftover cooked chicken in the fridge, this makes a great after-school or -college instant-energy snack.

You can use a pizza wheel to slice the finished quesadilla into triangles, which also travel well, stacked and wrapped in foil. **Feeds 4 fledglings**

8 soft white tortilla wraps
300 g grated mature Cheddar cheese
250 g cooked chicken, chopped into small pieces
4 spring onions, finely chopped
4 Peppadews®, drained and finely chopped
60 ml (4 Tbsp) sour cream
Salt and freshly ground black pepper
20 ml (4 tsp) olive oil

Lay out four of the tortillas and scatter half the grated cheese evenly over the wraps.

Sprinkle over the cooked chicken, spring onions and Peppadews®. Finish by adding the rest of the grated cheese, and smooth out until everything is evenly distributed.

Lay out the four remaining tortillas and spread 15 ml (1 Tbsp) of the sour cream over each one. Season with salt and pepper and then place them, sour cream side down, on top of the existing cheese-covered wraps.

Heat a large frying pan, big enough to take the whole wrap without folding it, and add 5 ml (1 tsp) of the oil. Carefully place a filled quesadilla in the pan and cook over a medium heat until it is crispy and the cheese is starting to melt. Check if the bottom of the quesadilla is cooked by lifting up a corner with a spatula. It should be golden, not blackened.

When the bottom is cooked, slide the whole tortilla onto a plate and cover tightly with another plate. Flip it over and slide back into the pan to cook the other side. When both sides are golden and the cheese has melted, it will be ready. Slide out onto a chopping board and cut into triangles (a pizza cutter does the job perfectly).

Repeat with the remaining quesadillas.

Carol's nanosecond cheese clouds

Everyone needs a friend like Carol. At her place, everyone's welcome, and grown-ups, children and assorted pets come, play and go all day long. With so much energy being expended, kids need regular feeding at short notice, which is when these irresistible cheesy clouds are invaluable. They're a bit like savoury muffins, but without the heavy cake-like texture.

The ingredients are all measured with one cup so kids can make their own, keeping them busy *and* well fed. I like to add a few extra fillings to make things interesting, but if you're dealing with linear, no-nonsense kids, step away from the green and stick to the cheese. **This recipe makes enough for a mini 12-hole muffin pan, but you'll almost certainly need more, so cut out the middle man and double it**

1 egg
80 ml (⅓ C) sunflower oil
250 ml (1 C) milk
250 ml (1 C) grated mature Cheddar cheese
250 ml (1 C) cake flour
Pinch of salt
10 ml (2 tsp) baking powder

Optional: 15 ml (1 Tbsp) finely chopped fresh chives
30 ml (2 Tbsp) finely chopped ham

Heat the oven to 220 °C. Line a mini 12-hole muffin pan with paper muffin cases or grease with nonstick food spray.

Whisk the egg, oil and milk together and stir in the cheese, plus the ham and chives if using.

Sift the flour, salt and baking powder together in a bowl.

Pour the wet, eggy mixture into the flour mix and stir well, then divide equally between the 12 paper muffin cases. Bake for 10 minutes, take out of the oven and cool until warm to touch.

These are best eaten straight away but, take it from me, that shouldn't prove a problem.

Broods on the run

Most of us spend an inordinate amount of time on the road, or on the run. We race around all week, and the weekends and holidays that used to provide valuable downtime seem to fill up far too quickly with matches, trips and visits. It's exhilarating but demanding, and apart from those rare moments when you're alone in the car, singing at the top of your lungs with a mug of coffee in hand, you'll probably be needing some help to keep you and everyone else going. The answer is to plan each trip with technical precision, and reduce the long journey whinge factor by allowing time for regular refuelling with a selection of tasty and diverting snacks.

Basic rules for good car food is that it should be healthy, interesting, preferably not sugary and although it's not worth being too precious about mess, preferably not flaky or dribbly. Self-contained meals in small parcels or portions work best and, after extensive road tests, I can safely say that the snatch-and-grab foods in this chapter are exceptionally effective. They can all be made in advance and are guaranteed to keep the inmates of your transporter well fed, happy and, hopefully, fairly quiet until you're nearly there.

Monster sausage roll

With just a few everyday ingredients, kids can produce this showstopper without your help. It is literally a big sausage roll, but unlike commercial horrors filled with pale unidentifiable mush, this uses apple, tomato and cheese to create an aromatic, flavour-packed parcel they'll want to make again and again.

At home, I would normally recommend that you ask your guests to sit down while the mini chef carries it aloft to the table, but as it makes the most amazing *padkos*, when you have the choice, take it to go. Sliced and wrapped in foil, dense and heavy with heat, it smells so amazing that even on a mammoth drive you'll soon have to screech to a halt for a happy munch.

For families or groups with a wide range of heat tolerances, make one end of the roll into a grown up spicy version and let the other end do the nursery. **Feeds 6**

2 eggs

8 good-quality big pork sausages or 450 g pork
   sausage meat

30 ml (2 Tbsp) tomato sauce

50 g Parmesan cheese, finely grated

15 ml (1 Tbsp) finely chopped fresh parsley

Optional: 2.5 ml (½ tsp) dried chilli flakes OR
   ¼ fresh red chilli, finely chopped

60 ml (4 Tbsp) apple sauce

Cake flour for dusting

1 x 400 g roll ready-made butter puff pastry

Heat the oven to 200 °C. Line a large baking tray with a sheet of greaseproof paper.

Beat 1 egg and tip it into a big mixing bowl. Squeeze the sausage meat out of the skins and add to the egg. Spoon in the tomato sauce, Parmesan cheese and parsley and stir to combine. If you're making a spicy end, split the mixture between two bowls and add the spicy bits to one bowl.

Flour your work surface well and roll out the puff pastry a little. Carefully lift it and place it on the lined baking tray. Spread the apple sauce in a 4-cm-wide line down the centre of the pastry, stopping 4 cm before the top and bottom edges. Spoon the sausage filling on top of the apple sauce, in a big sausage shape. Leave room at each side and a gap at the top and bottom of about 4 cm each. Season well with salt and black pepper.

Now you're going to plait your monster. Starting 2 cm from the line of sausage in the middle, cut the pastry on each side of the sausage into diagonal strips about 2 cm wide. Beat the remaining egg and paint all the strips with a thin layer of egg wash. Fold the top and bottom strips of pastry over the top and bottom of the sausage mixture. Then, starting at the top, make a plait by taking a strip from one side and laying it over the filling, followed by the strip on the other side. It should make a tight, even plait. Keep plaiting down to the bottom of the pastry, making sure none of the filling shows through, as it will leak out and ruin the look of your roll.

Brush the whole roll with the rest of the egg and pop the tray into the centre of the oven. Bake for 35 minutes or until puffy and golden. Take out and serve hot or, if you're in a rush to get going, let it cool slightly, then carefully cut into big slices. Hold them all together so it looks as if the roll is still intact, wrap tightly in two layers of foil, and hit the road.

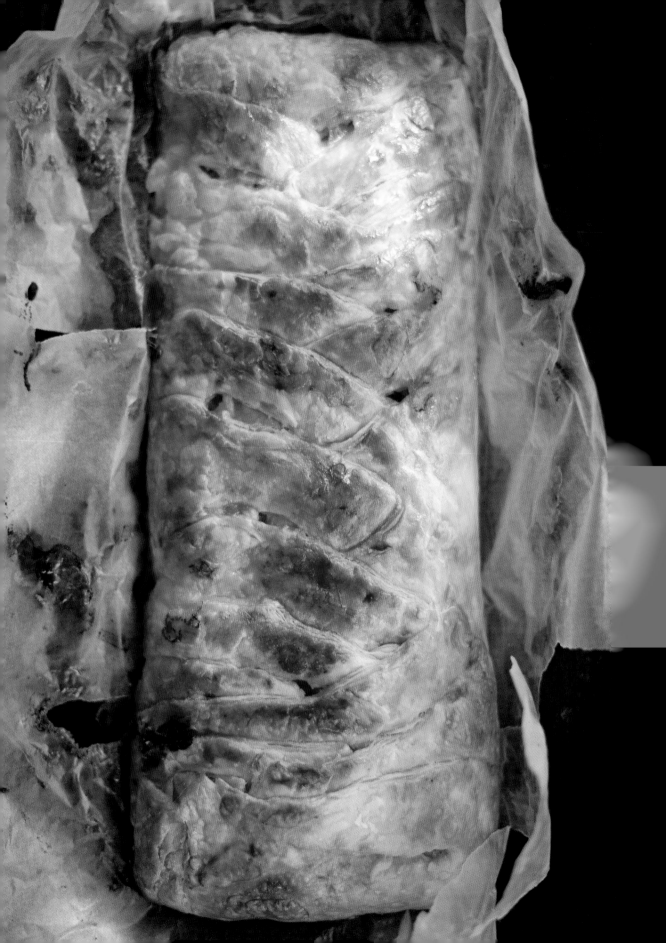

Pavement special sandwich

A 'pavement special' is what we call our much-loved hound, who was, predictably, the first dog we saw at the rescue shelter. Like many street dogs, she had been concocted from multiple breeds, all of which came joyfully together in an impossibly cute doggie package, and it was mutual love and slavish adoration at first sight.

Which is a lot like this recipe. It started out life as a school project to create the ultimate sandwich, and quickly moved up the food chain to become our favourite picnic fodder. The ingredients seem like a random jumble of deli goodies, but the tastes and textures are chosen for their ability to meld beautifully together into a whole meal. Use a sturdy bread loaf, like sourdough, which is tougher and copes well with moisture, and preferably in an old-fashioned cottage loaf shape, so when it's cooked, you can cut everyone satisfyingly fat wedges.

Kids love mini-versions too, which you can make with round crusty rolls. Both shapes travel well and make excellent packed lunches. **Feeds 6**

1 medium, round loaf of bread
75 ml (5 Tbsp) butter
100 g Cheddar cheese, thinly sliced
5 slices Parma ham or prosciutto
1 large handful fresh rocket
10 thin slices chorizo or salami

8 large sun-dried tomatoes in oil, drained and
    finely chopped
1 large handful fresh basil leaves
100 g mozzarella cheese, thinly sliced
5 ml (1 tsp) chopped fresh chives
Salt and freshly ground black pepper

Slice a thick 'lid' off the top of the loaf – it needs to be the width of the whole loaf, not just a little lid from the very top. Carefully cut out the inside of the loaf, leaving the bottom intact and a thick crust all the way round. Slice the piece you have cut out in half horizontally so you have a round slice of bread and set it aside. Butter the inside of the loaf and the lid.

Fill the loaf from the bottom to the top, by first covering the base of the hollowed-out loaf with a layer of Cheddar slices, then adding half of the following ingredients in layers: Parma ham/prosciutto, rocket, chorizo/salami, Cheddar, chopped sun-dried tomatoes, basil leaves and mozzarella. Sprinkle with half of the chopped chives. Add one of the thin slices of bread you have left over from the middle of the loaf, season well and start with the layers again until you reach the top. End with a layer of cheese.

The loaf should be tightly filled, but since they do differ in size, add a few more layers if it is not full. When you can't fit in another thing, pop the bread 'lid' on top and wrap the whole loaf neatly in greaseproof or baking paper. Tie it up tightly, parcel style, with old-fashioned string so that it compacts the filling. When you are ready to eat, preheat the oven to 190 °C, place the loaf on a lightly floured baking tray and bake for 20 minutes to melt the cheese.

Serve immediately or slice into thick wedges and then wrap in several layers of foil if you're heading out.

Mini scotch eggs with harissa mayonnaise

Blindly revering old recipes out of nostalgia can be a disaster (blancmange anyone?) and when it comes to Scotch eggs, I don't have the happiest of memories. Dusty eggs encircled by ominous grey rings and texture-less pink spam, and spray blasted with orange breadcrumbs, were never a good idea. But here, with a little downsizing and a lot of revitalising, they are a complete revelation.

Quails' eggs make perfect bite-sized munchies, but wrap them in quality sausage meat and you'll have the ideal retro-tastic picnic food. They take longer to make than a sandwich, but if you can bear to not eat them straight away, they will keep happily in the ubiquitous foil package until it's time to throw them to the hungry hordes in the back seat. **Makes 12**

12 quails' eggs
5 ml (1 tsp) finely chopped fresh parsley or
   6 fresh sage leaves, finely chopped
½ chargrilled red pepper from a jar (see
   page 115), very finely chopped
5 ml (1 tsp) tomato paste
400 g pork sausage meat
Salt and freshly ground black pepper

60 ml (4 Tbsp) cake flour seasoned with a little
   salt and pepper
2 eggs, beaten
100 g croutons, blitzed to crumbs
Vegetable oil for deep-frying

To serve
2.5 ml (½ tsp) Hellishly hot harissa (see page 54)
   mixed with 45 ml (3 Tbsp) mayonnaise

Bring a small saucepan of water to the boil, place the quails' eggs in the pan and boil for 3 minutes. They do break easily, so be gentle. Remove and place in a pan of cold water.

Mix the parsley or sage, red pepper and tomato paste together, then add the sausage meat and mix well before seasoning. If you have used sausage meat rather than sausages, you will need to season more generously. Peel the quails' eggs. The easiest way is to roll them on a hard surface so the shell cracks everywhere, then you should be able to take the shell off in strips.

Split the sausage mixture into 12 equal-sized pieces. Take a piece of sausage meat in your hand, flatten it in your palm and place the quails' egg in the centre. Carefully work the meat around the egg evenly so you can't see any white, then set aside. Repeat the process with the remaining eggs and meat.

Lay out three bowls. Fill one with the seasoned flour, the next bowl with the beaten eggs and the third bowl with the pulverised croutons. Roll the sausage-covered egg lightly in the flour, then the egg and finish with an even coating of ground croutons.

Heat a small saucepan and fill it to a third of the way up with vegetable oil. Heat the oil. When a small piece of sausage meat fries quickly and floats up to the top, the oil is ready. Carefully place the Scotch eggs into the hot oil (you will probably need to do this in batches depending on the size of your saucepan) and fry until golden and crispy all over. It will take about 10 minutes with the first batch and less with the other batches as the oil gets hotter. Remove with a slotted spoon and place on kitchen paper to absorb any excess oil. Allow to cool and then serve with the harissa mayonnaise.

Speedy spanokopitas

The joy of spanokopita lies in the coming together of salty, tangy feta and earthy spinach, which makes for a divinely dense filling wrapped up in crisp golden packaging. Making them also gives you the opportunity to say 'spanokopita' a lot, which I love.

Tongue twisters aside, these classic Greek snacks are extremely useful and not as fiddly to produce as you may think. Phyllo pastry has had a bad press, but although you're supposed to keep the sheets damp, it doesn't seem to matter if you work fast, which you will, after a teeny bit of practice. Enlist the kids, as they're super quick to catch on to packaging techniques, and you can use the exercise for Maths revision. Get them to weigh out the fillings, then do a quick geometry lesson as they fold and roll the neat triangles.

Spanokopita make great snacks or light lunches, but as food for kids they come into their own when you're on the run. Wrap them in foil to hand them out in the car when everyone's bored and whiney and you'll buy yourself a good 15 minutes of peace. **Makes 8–10**

200 g spinach, washed and drained
10 ml (2 tsp) butter
1 small onion, finely chopped
200 g feta cheese, crumbled
2 eggs, beaten
30 ml (2 Tbsp) chopped fresh dill

Salt and freshly ground black pepper
30 ml (2 Tbsp) grated Parmesan cheese
120 g phyllo pastry
100 g butter, melted
5 ml (1 tsp) sesame seeds

Heat the oven to 190 °C.

Cook the spinach in a pan with 5 ml (1 tsp) of the butter until wilted. Remove, drain and chop finely. Set aside.

Fry the chopped onion in another 5 ml (1 tsp) of butter until transparent. Allow to cool.

Mix the chopped, drained spinach with the onion, feta, eggs and dill, and season with salt and pepper. Sprinkle over the Parmesan and mix in.

Lay out the phyllo pastry and cut lengthways into strips 10 cm wide. Brush melted butter over a strip of pastry. Spoon 15 ml (1 Tbsp) of the spinach mixture onto the pastry strip, 2 cm from the bottom. Fold the bottom right corner of the strip over the filling and up to the left to make a triangle, then fold over again to make another triangle. Continue folding to the top of the strip. You should have a neat triangular package. Place onto a greased baking sheet.

Butter the next pastry strip and start again. Keep going until you have used up the filling mixture. Brush the triangles with melted butter and scatter with a few sesame seeds. Bake for 15–20 minutes until golden and leave to cool a little before eating.

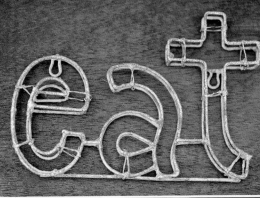

Sweetness

Perhaps because it's just a little bit naughty, the first taste of a beautiful cake always takes me back to school camps and wonderfully illicit midnight feasts. Usually planned days in advance and with military precision, the rare occasions when we managed to make it until midnight were unforgettable, filled as they were with sugar-fuelled abandon and heart-stopping excitement.

Now I dutifully try to save sweet things for special moments, but if they don't come around fast enough, I've found that tea time is always a good reason to start baking. And since I've had children it's been even easier, as their handily heightened sense of occasion means even one cupcake can make a party. It's a win-win – I get to fill my kitchen with snow-white icing sugar clouds and cute, floury-nosed bakers, and the kids couldn't be happier. Even better, the sweet stuff is always edible, so every baking session is guaranteed to be a success. It's the perfect introduction to cooking and the feeling of pride kids get from producing a wobbly cake or a plateful of crumbly biscuits creates indelible memories for even the littlest bakers.

For adults, baking is the ultimate therapy in demanding times. What could be better for the soul than a house swirling with heady wafts of vanilla, chocolate and cinnamon? With a cake warm and snug in the oven, the world suddenly becomes a lighter, happier place, filled with delicious anticipation of good things to come.

Above all, sugary treats are the perfect reason to sit down and share good things with the people you love, whether it's a friend in need of tea and sympathy or a gloriously indulgent birthday party. Use any excuse, and big it up with these beautiful bakes.

Auntie Gladys's fork biscuits

Auntie Gladys was my absurdly perfect great aunt. A skinny, sprightly spinster with impeccable posture, she was also an independent woman who worked in the local jam factory for 40 years, and in her eighties was still cycling every week to the local market to sell flowers from her garden.

Visits to her cottage never felt like a duty because she adored the company of children and was wonderfully indulgent. Afternoon tea was always served on exquisitely embroidered linen tablecloths, with strong tea in delicate china for the parents and orange squash for us. We climbed trees in the garden and ate scones with lots of jam (thanks to her connections), and my favourite fork biscuits, which melted on your tongue with a sugary kick.

I asked for the recipe as a teenager and it arrived on the back of a crimped Christmas card (she was a great recycler) in shaky copperplate handwriting. Auntie Gladys never left England in her lifetime, but I know she would be tickled pink to know that her great and great-great nieces are still making these biscuits on the other side of the world. **Makes 15–20 biscuits**

110 g margarine or butter, at room
    temperature
50 g castor sugar, plus extra for
    sprinkling
2.5 ml (½ tsp) vanilla or almond
    essence
150 g self-raising flour

Heat the oven to 180 °C.

Cream the margarine or butter and sugar until light and fluffy. Stir in the vanilla essence and gradually mix in the flour. Roll the mixture into small balls then place them on a baking sheet lined with greaseproof paper and flatten with a wet fork.

Bake for 15–20 minutes until lightly golden, then sprinkle with castor sugar while still hot. Leave to cool for 10 minutes then remove and place on a cooling rack.

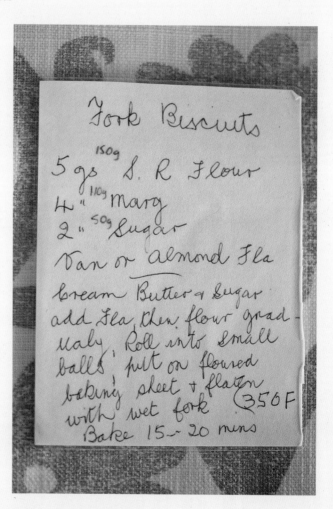

Tra-la-la tiara biscuits

If you only buy one biscuit cutter in your life, please make it tiara-shaped. After years of using all shapes and sizes, this never fails to bring out the most creative streaks in little bakers.

If it's princess heaven you're looking for, it makes a perfect tiara just asking to be painted with rosy pink icing, and if it's world domination you're after, the same cutter makes a fine crown for boys and girls, allowing the decorator to top each prong with suitably vulgar fake jewels and dust with clouds of priceless gold and silver glitter. Whoever's baking, I guarantee you'll end up with fabulously bejewelled biscuits to rival Aladdin's cave.

This vanilla dough recipe is the same one I've used since I was a child. It's foolproof and can be frozen at the dough stage if you ever have time for forward planning. Thaw first before baking. **Makes approximately 20 tiara or crown biscuits, depending how big your cutter (and your head) is**

225 g butter, at room temperature
125 g castor sugar (vanilla sugar if you have it)
2.5 ml (½ tsp) vanilla essence
1 egg yolk, beaten
325 g cake flour
Coloured water icing
Decorations: sweets, sprinkles, edible glitter, sugar

Heat the oven to 180 °C. Grease a couple of baking trays.

Cream the butter, then add the castor sugar and beat until light and fluffy. Add the vanilla essence and egg yolk before sifting in the flour and mixing well. You should have a firm dough that is smooth enough to handle. If it is too dry, add a little milk, and if too wet, add a little more flour.

Spilt the dough in half, cover half in plastic wrap and put it in the fridge until you need to make another batch. Lightly flour a surface and roll out the remaining half of dough. If it's looking sticky, roll it out between two pieces of baking paper.

Get out your best cutters and set the kids to work, creating their dream tiaras and crowns. Place the biscuits on the greased baking trays and bake for 10–12 minutes or until golden.

Remove from the oven and cool on wire racks before the kids ice and decorate the biscuits in the sparkliest, glitteriest, loudest and tackiest way they can. None of that 'less is more' business here.

Labryinth biscuits

If you're over 12 years old, these are mildly interesting vanilla and chocolate shortbreads, but if you're under 12, they are quite impossible to eat normally. The problem is that these simple biscuits make the perfect edible game. You'll begin by nibbling around the different colours, and won't be able to stop until all that's left is a single-coloured microdot, perfectly sized to snaffle in one bite and hopefully bigger than your friend's.

To make it even more fun for the kids, increase the size of the roll, which will create big, slightly trippy, Alice in Wonderland-esque biscuits. You could also use a couple of drops of food colouring instead of cocoa to make half of the dough bright green, blue or red.

Making them is easier than you would think, just requiring a steady hand and a touch of mathematical precision to shape and work the dough. **This makes 16 small biscuits**

100 g cake flour
50 g cornflour
15 ml (1 Tbsp) cocoa powder
100 g butter, at room temperature
50 g castor sugar
10 ml (2 tsp) vanilla essence
15 ml (1 Tbsp) milk

Sift the flour and cornflour together, then divide equally into two bowls. Add the cocoa powder to one bowl to make the chocolate mix, then set both bowls aside.

Cream the butter, sugar and vanilla essence together until pale and fluffy. Divide into two and add each half to a bowl of flour mixture. Knead the ingredients of each bowl to make two smooth balls of dough. Wrap each one in plastic wrap and refrigerate for 1 hour.

Roll out each piece of dough separately between two pieces of greaseproof paper into a rectangle about 25 x 15 cm. Brush a little milk over one of the layers of dough and place the second layer directly on top. Roll up carefully, starting from the longer edge, to make a log shape. Wrap tightly in plastic wrap and chill in the fridge for another 30 minutes.

Heat the oven to 180 °C. Grease a large baking tray.

Remove the plastic wrap and cut gently into 16 slices, taking care not to squash the log as you cut. Place the biscuits on the baking tray and bake for 15–20 minutes. Remove and cool on a rack before eating.

Huge chocolate buttons

Maximum chocolate gratification for minimal effort makes this my default rainy day recipe. All you're doing is melting and reforming chocolate, but making monster chocolate buttons as big as saucers (instead of packets of measly chocolate spots from packets) is outrageously good fun for kids of any age.

Decorations should be brash, so dig out everything sprinkly, glittery or brightly coloured and made of sugar and hand it over to your cooks. And if you don't think kids should have all the fun, whip up some after-midnight buttons using dark, dark chocolate sprinkled in a sophisticated fashion with crystallised ginger, peppermint crystals or shreds of gold leaf. **Makes 20–30 buttons, depending on who is cooking, and how excited they get**

300 g milk, white or dark chocolate, broken into squares
For decoration: sprinkles, glitter, smarties, crystallised ginger, peppermint crystals, gold leaf
You'll also need a clean pastry brush or a very clean paintbrush

Bring a saucepan of water to the boil, then turn down to the merest simmer. Place the chocolate pieces in a heatproof glass bowl and place over the saucepan, making sure it doesn't actually touch the water. Allow the chocolate to melt, stirring as little as possible.

Tear off a big sheet of baking paper and lay flat, using weights at each end to hold it down. Place a small glass or mug on the paper and draw a pencil line around it to make your button shapes. Turn the paper over so you can still see the circles and weigh down again.

When the chocolate has melted, drop a spoonful into the middle of each faint circle and use the brush to paint the chocolate outwards to the edge of the circles.

While the chocolate is still wet, scatter over decorations and sprinkles. They will catch and settle in the melted chocolate. Leave to harden, or if it's a hot day, slide the paper carefully onto a baking tray and put it into the fridge. When the buttons have set, carefully peel off the paper and eat.

Sixties bull's-eye shortbread lollipops

Like many of the best recipes, this came about by mistake. Trying to recreate a girly vision of heart lollipops from a magazine turned into a disaster. The shortbread leaked in the oven like a ripe cheese and the icing was as mean and thin as a bowl of gruel.

But rather than bin the results, we experimented with some mad icing colours, dripping one on top of the other, and suddenly it all fell into place in a sixties, bull's-eye, retro fashion. The kids thought they were awesome, and a party favourite was born, although now I use my own trusty lollipop recipe to ensure they keep their shape. **This will make 8–10 lollipops**

220 g salted butter, at room temperature
125 g castor sugar
1 tiny drop vanilla essence
275 g cake flour
50 g cornflour
8–10 wooden lollipop sticks (or kebab sticks with the points cut off, and any splintery bits removed)
100 g icing sugar
5 ml (1 tsp) water
3 different food colourings

Beat the butter and castor sugar in a large bowl until fluffy. Add the vanilla essence and mix well. Stir in the two sifted flours and knead to a smooth dough. Roll into a thick sausage shape and, without squashing it, cover in plastic wrap and refrigerate for 1 hour.

Heat the oven to 180 °C. Grease a baking tray.

Remove the dough from the fridge, take off the plastic wrap and slice the dough into rounds about 1 cm thick. Place the rounds on the baking tray with plenty of space between, then gently slide a lollipop stick into each biscuit. Make sure you can't see the stick on either side of the dough circle. Bake for 25–30 minutes until golden. Remove and leave to cool.

While the biscuits cool, make the icing. It needs to be dribbly enough to drop off a spoon but not so much that it will completely slide off the biscuit. Divide the icing into three separate bowls and add your chosen colours to each one. When the lollipops have cooled, drop a tablespoon of icing onto each biscuit. When that has started to set a little, drop half a tablespoon of the next colour into the middle. It should spread out a little but you should still be able to see the first colour around the edges. Continue with a teaspoon of the third colour.

Leave the icing to set completely before presenting the finished lollies to your eager guests.

Chocolate and hot mint slices

Mint and dark chocolate are always good together, but throw in a crunchy biscuit base and you'll have an irresistible traybake that is a hot, minty cross between millionaire's shortbread and hiker's mint cake. Great for afternoon tea or in teeny squares as pudding after a big supper. They look even better if you add some bling with a dusting of edible gold glitter. **Makes 20 luxurious and very naughty squares**

120 g salted butter, at room temperature
100 g castor sugar
200 g cake flour
250 g icing sugar
5 ml (1 tsp) peppermint essence
Optional: green food colouring
300 g dark chocolate
Edible gold glitter for dusting

Heat the oven to 180 °C.

Mix the butter and sugar together until pale and fluffy. Gradually add the flour and mix until it forms a dough. It will be very crumbly, but pull it together as best you can and press into a square 20 cm baking tin. Smooth the dough so that it is level and even. Prick gently with a fork and bake for 10–15 minutes until just golden. Take out and leave to cool.

Meanwhile, make the peppermint filling by mixing the icing sugar with a little water to make a smooth paste, then add the peppermint essence. Add a few drops of green food colouring if you prefer the icing to look mintier, and spread on top of the biscuit base.

Break the chocolate into squares and melt gently over a pan of simmering water, trying not to stir. When it's melted, pour the chocolate over the peppermint icing and cut into slices or squares in the tin before the chocolate sets. Dust with edible glitter.

Mum's cornflake cracklet cakes

Thank you to the genius who discovered that cornflakes and chocolate made music together. Every birthday, I thank them, and Mum, who made sure they were present at every party. The alchemy between the crunchy flakes, syrup and cocoa creates a softly chewy biscuit/cake crossbreed that is so irresistible that no party has happened in our house without a parent asking for the recipe.

You'll mostly need store cupboard ingredients to turn out a perfect batch, which is particularly useful if your kids come home and announce it's bake sale, market day, or someone's birthday tomorrow and it will be the end of the world if they don't have a tray of cakes to carry proudly aloft into school. Even better, they are ridiculously easy to make so tell them it's fine, as long as they make the cakes themselves...

Three generations of our family now make these, each adding their own twists. My daughter favours the addition of sprinkles and glitter, Mum pours the whole recipe into a small cake tin, and cuts it like a cake when it sets, while I am the purist who makes them just like this. If you use margarine instead of butter, the recipe is gluten and dairy free, so friends with allergies can munch away happily too. **Makes 12 small cakes or one round**

60 g margarine or butter (NB: do not use soft margarine from a tub,
   it needs to be block margarine or butter)
30 ml (2 Tbsp) icing sugar
30 ml (2 Tbsp) golden syrup
30 ml (2 Tbsp) cocoa powder
60 g cornflakes

Melt the margarine or butter, icing sugar and syrup together in a saucepan over low heat until merged. Don't let it boil. Remove from the heat, add the cocoa and mix in gently. Fold in the cornflakes until completely covered. Pour into small paper cupcake cases or a greased and lined 23 cm sandwich tin. Leave to set in the fridge before serving.

National treasure apple cake

My mum has always been a baker and her gorgeously aromatic, legendary apple cake is straight out of central casting. Incredibly moist and heavy in a golden, sweet, delightfully stodgy way, it definitely deserves its national treasure status.

When I need a quick present for a friend, or there's a panic for a pud, this culinary staple is the one I turn to. It's the perfect cake for two reasons. Firstly, it looks amazing no matter what you do to it. I've taught this recipe to kids, non-baking blokes and a pensioner who had never baked before, yet each time the result was picture perfect. Secondly, it requires only a few, humdrum ingredients which you probably have in your kitchen already, so no expensive deli trips or mad dashes to the supermarket.

Just be aware that this is a self-contained type of cake, not prone to big explosions because of the weight of the apples, so don't be alarmed when it doesn't rise very much. As with politicians, what you lose in hot air you generally gain in integrity. **Feeds 8**

175 g butter or margarine (it's not fussy), at room temperature
175 g castor sugar
3 large eggs
175 g self-raising flour
1 ml (¼ tsp) ground cinnamon
4 medium apples (normal eating apples are fine; do not used tinned apples), peeled, cored and
  thinly sliced
15 ml (1 Tbsp) castor sugar mixed with 1 ml (¼ tsp) ground cinnamon for sprinkling over the top,
  plus extra for serving

Heat the oven to 170 °C. Grease and line a 24 cm round cake tin. I've made this in different size tins and they all worked so don't worry if you haven't got exactly the right size. You can also use a loaf tin, but it's not as pretty.

Cream the butter and sugar together until light and fluffy. You can do this by hand or with a mixer. Add the eggs and mix in well. Stir in the sifted flour and cinnamon and stir until blended. Gently fold in the sliced apples.

Pour the batter into the cake tin and sprinkle the castor sugar and cinnamon mixture evenly over the top. Bake for 50–60 minutes until lightly golden on top. Test with a skewer to see that it's cooked inside.

Leave to cool in the tin for at least 30 minutes and dredge with a little more cinnamon sugar before serving.

Million-dollar movie star marshmallow cake

Adding a packet of jelly to a cake mixture feels wrong on so many levels, but if you need a centrepiece to a gloriously pink and frivolous girly event, this glamorous, scene stealer of a cake is it. Here, blackcurrant jelly crystals create a beautiful pale pink-mauve sponge reminiscent of tea roses in an old-fashioned flower garden (so tricky to achieve with food colouring). Saving a few crystals for the topping means you can crown your creation with a rosy, sticky-sweet meringue and marshmallow icing, which lurches and lolls crazily yet miraculously always manages to stop at the edges of your cake.

This cake is not your common or garden sponge and requires time, love and effort but, like a movie star, perfect packages don't come cheap. Plus, it's so pretty, I defy you not to look at it without smiling. **Feeds 10 people a big, fat slice each**

Sponge base
220 g self-raising flour
45 ml (3 Tbsp) blackcurrant flavoured jelly
   crystals
220 g butter, at room temperature
220 g castor sugar
4 eggs
15 ml (1 Tbsp) milk

Icing
250 g castor sugar
The rest of the packet of jelly crystals
2 egg whites
65 ml water
1 ml (¼ tsp) cream of tartar

Heat the oven to 180 °C. Grease two 20 cm sandwich tins.

To make the sponge, sift the flour and jelly crystals together. The jelly will be hard to push through the sieve, but rub as much through as you can before throwing away any particularly stubborn crystals.

Beat the butter until creamy, then add the castor sugar gradually until the mixture goes pale and fluffy. Beat in the eggs, one at a time, adding a spoonful of flour if it looks like it wants to curdle. Fold in the flour and jelly mixture, and the milk, but don't knock out the air as you want the cake as light as possible. Divide the mixture evenly between the greased tins and bake for 20 minutes until risen and springy. When the sponges are ready, leave to cool before removing from their tins.

While the sponges are baking, make the icing. It's fiddly but worth it. Boil some water in a small saucepan, then turn down the heat to a simmer. Put a glass heatproof bowl over the pan and add all the icing ingredients. As it simmers, carefully whisk with a hand-held electric mixer until the mixture is like a thick meringue and holds its shape. It may take a while but it will happen.

Spread a third of the icing over one sponge. Gently place the other sponge on top, and artfully dollop on the rest of the icing, letting it spread out wherever it fancies.

This cake looks good all by itself, but I usually can't resist sprinkling over a few silver balls and a dusting of glitter. Alternatively, use pre-made perfect icing flowers.

Omg super short apple pie

After a pile of windfall apples had been staring at me balefully for a week, I was shamed into doing the decent thing. This messy, crumbly, broken-up state of affairs was what came along. It won't win any pastry beauty contests, but the combination of melt-in-the-mouth pastry and sharp apples (for this is no sickly sweet affair) is so delicious that you'll find your guests will go silent after the first mouthful, lost in the moment. For elderly friends or family, this pie takes them back to times when life was somehow simpler. The young ones will wonder why we don't eat more pies. Cook for pudding after Sunday lunch, or for afternoon tea after a lazy walk. **Feeds 8**

Pastry
225 g butter, at room temperature
50 g castor sugar, plus extra for dusting
2 eggs
350 g cake flour

Filling
1.2 kg cooking apples
100 g soft brown sugar
2.5 ml (½ tsp) ground cinnamon
2.5 ml (½ tsp) ground mixed spice
30 ml (2 Tbsp) cake flour

First, make the pastry. I use a food processor, because I am lazy, and it works. Place the softened butter and castor sugar in the processor and blitz until combined. Add 1 whole egg, and 1 yolk, keeping the second egg white for glazing later.

Gradually add the cake flour. When it starts to clump together, scrape it out of the processor and collect the bits into a smooth-ish ball of dough. Cover the ball in plastic wrap and stick in the fridge for 45 minutes while you make the filling.

Peel, core and cut the apples into thick slices. Toss them in a bowl with the soft brown sugar and add the spices and flour, stirring through well.

Preheat the oven to 180 °C. Grease a pie dish. Mine is 23 cm but you can use sizes from 20 to 25 cm.

Remove the chilled pastry from the fridge, cut off a third, cover it in plastic wrap and set aside. Roll out the remaining dough on a floured surface, then cut into a circle and use it to line the pie dish. Let the dough hang over the sides a little.

Tip the apple filling on top of the pastry, then use the small ball of dough to make a lid. Squeeze the top and sides of the dough together to seal, then gently shave off any overhang. Use the tines of a fork to press little lines around the edges of the pie.

Roll out your extra scraps of dough and use it to make words or shapes to decorate the top of the pie, then beat the remaining egg white and use it to wash the pie.

Make four or five little knife slashes in the pastry to let the steam out, sprinkle with a generous dusting of castor sugar and bake for 40–45 minutes.

Check to see that it is golden and bubbling, take out and leave to cool, but not before giving it an extra dredging of castor sugar while it's still hot. Serve hot, cold or standing on your head. It's going to taste amazing whatever.

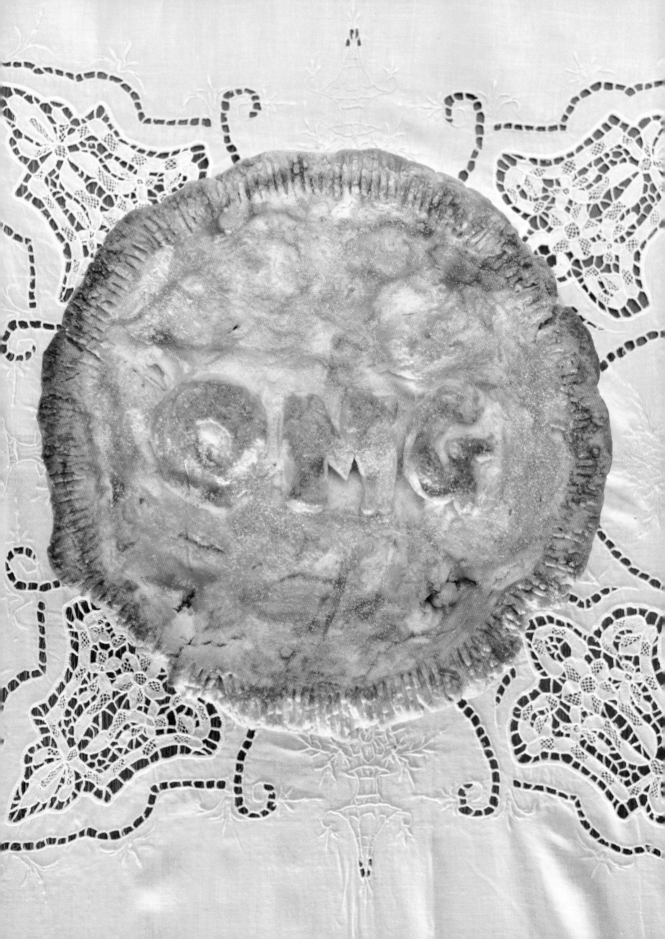

A small, but perfectly formed mango and lime sorbet (with optional vodka)

Sometimes you need just the teeniest mouthful of something sweet. After a huge lunch perhaps, when there's little space for stodge, or on one of those scorching summer days when it's too hot to move.

Every spoonful of this classic sorbet tastes like a dream and you don't need an ice-cream maker as it can be made in any shallow dish. The vodka isn't compulsory, but it stops the sorbet from freezing rock solid. That's my story anyway. **Feeds 4**

2 x 410 tins mango slices, drained
125 ml (½ C) sugar
60 ml (4 Tbsp) water
15 ml (1 Tbsp) vodka
Zest of 1 lime
Juice of ½ lime

In a food processor, blitz the mango slices to a pulp and then pour into a shallow, freezerproof serving bowl.

Place the sugar and water in a small saucepan over a low heat and warm, stirring gently, until the sugar has dissolved and the liquid is clear. Pour the liquid over the mango pulp and mix well. Stir in the vodka, the lime zest and juice. Place the bowl in the freezer.

After 1 hour, remove and stir well, then replace. It is ready as soon as it has frozen, just take it out a few minutes before serving to defrost slightly.

Recipe index